A D O N I S   C E L E S T I N E

Quality Engineering:
The Missing Key to Digital CX

Tools for sharpening the quality and reliability of the customer experience in the digital marketplace

Table of Contents

ABOUT THE AUTHOR

Adonis Celestine

Director of Automation, Applause

Adonis is an automation expert, QA thought leader, e-book author and regular speaker at leading software testing conferences. He has 18 years of experience in the IT industry in a variety of roles involving building, testing and selling software. He received a Bachelor of Engineering degree from the Government College of Engineering and an MBA from the Symbiosis Institute. He currently leads the test automation practice at Applause.

Technology is a passion for Adonis, and he believes that true quality is a collective perspective of customer experiences. Also, he thinks the natural evolution of QA is shaped by data and machine intelligence. Adonis's quest to look at the quality challenges of the modern world through different lenses and address them through innovative and unconventional methods led to the genesis of this book. You can find him online at LinkedIn @ AdonisCelestine.

ACKNOWLEDGEMENTS

I am extremely grateful to my parents Mr Celestine and Mrs Jesi for their loving care and sacrifices for educating and preparing me for my future. I am very thankful to my wife - Cerena, daughter - Louvina and son - Leandro for their understanding and continuous support to complete this book.

I would also like to acknowledge and give my warmest thanks to:

Marco Kortman, who made this book possible. His guidance and advice carried me through all the stages of writing. Thanks for being there from day one of ideation to the completion of the book.

Feline Schäffers , the greatest designer I could ever imagine who is responsible for the cover design and wonderful graphics in the book.

Andreas Golze, for his amazing leadership and guidance during my time at Cognizant.

Saksham Sarode for being a great mentor and sharp reviewer of the book and its ideas.

Iram Verburg, for being a great friend, and offering intellectual insights, recommendations and brilliant thoughts. Thanks extra for helping with the Short bytes.

Without the experiences and support from colleagues at Cognizant, this book would not exist. Additional thanks to my Cognizant colleagues Alan Alper, Aman Jaggi, Anand Soosai and Rohit Sinha.

PREFACE

We see our customers as invited guests to a party, and we are the hosts. It's our job every day to make every important aspect of the customer experience a little bit better.[1] — Jeff Bezos, Entrepreneur, Investor

-- -- -- -- -- -- -- -- --

Today's exponential shifts in technological innovation have radically changed how businesses operate and interact with customers. But despite the seismic disruptions of our increasingly digitized world, the fundamental principle of being *customer-centric* to be a success in business remains in effect — in fact, it's stronger than ever.

What *has* changed, in fact, is that customers have become increasingly demanding in the modern, digital era, as their expectations have been cultivated through exceptional experiences in shopping, buying, communication, etc. With competition looming — most of it digital-native — businesses must make every interaction with the customer count.

One facet of the evolution we are seeing is that interaction touchpoints have changed dramatically, from physical store predominance to the proliferation of digital options such as online stores, social media, mobile commerce, digital assistants, etc.

With such an increase in the number of touchpoints — and the associated hypergrowth in data streams — marketing focus has shifted from products per se to user experiences. In fact, according to industry analysts,[2] customer experience will be the key differentiator in a post pandemic world.

1   https://yourstory.com/2020/01/jeff-bezos-quotes-amazon-ceo-founder-birthday/amp
2   https://www.forrester.com/press-newsroom/forresters-us-2020-customer-experience-index-reveals-cx-quality-improved-dramatically-over-the-past-year/

> *"You're no longer selling products, you are selling experiences."[3]*

We see *customer experience* — the product of all interactions that a customer has with an organization across all touchpoints — as *the conversation between your product or service and the customer*. The key is keeping these conversations interesting and rewarding. If the conversation bores them, your customers will leave and talk to a more interesting competitor. The way to keep the customer interested is to make their life simpler, better and easier with human-centric products and services.

For quality assurance purposes, this human- and customer-centric focus requires an important perspective shift, from the traditional paradigm centered on product features and functionality to the new hyperattention on providing the right customer experience at every step of the process.

To become laser-focused on customer experience, numerous questions must be answered:

- *What is the right level of experience?*
- *How can we ensure the quality of customer experience?*
- *Can we assure the same experience across channels?*
- *How can we control the experience provided by machine intelligence?*
- *Is our quality assurance strategy equipped to handle machine intelligence?*

This book will help you answer these and many other related questions. It will provide you with practical examples and methodologies for developing state-of-the-art customer experience assurance, by deploying the cutting-edge technologies shaping the industry such as machine learning and other AI applications.

---

3   *https://mention.com/en/blog/selling-product-experiences/*

Enhancing customer experience is impossible without assuring 100% reliability and repeatability. Quality assurance is a critical function throughout the product/service ecosystem, the key process that will determine whether your consumers are satisfied or disappointed. This book is aimed at enabling you to take your modern organization into the user-centric future.

READER'S GUIDE

This book is for anyone who is seeking to learn how ensuring quality creates an unmatched customer experience.

- - - - - - - - - - - - - - - - - -

Our book is divided into three parts, each of which covers a different level of engagement in customer experiences from a quality point of view. The three levels are experiences that appeal, experiences that delight and experiences that "wow."

Part I covers experiences that appeal enough to a customer to impel engagement with a company or product. Company reputation, perception of privacy, security and product performance are all potential factors influencing this type of appeal.

Part II concerns experiences that delight a customer, such as continuously impressing users with new or improved features and providing a seamless experience across all devices. Such activities provide a higher level of user satisfaction that helps businesses keep customers satisfied and loyal.

Part III treats experiences that induce a "wow"-like response from users, such as personalized service, a sense of contribution to the product's development or other bonding experiences. This is how true and enduring customer loyalty is established for the company and/or the product.

Each part comprises four chapters, each of which with three sections: an introduction, mindshare about the topic and a discussion of quality aspects. We also include "Short Bytes" throughout the book to showcase some fun facts.

Exhibit 1 depicts the three steps of CX that we used to organize this book, including a sampling of quality techniques applicable with each stage.

Exhibit 1: Customer experience assurance catalog

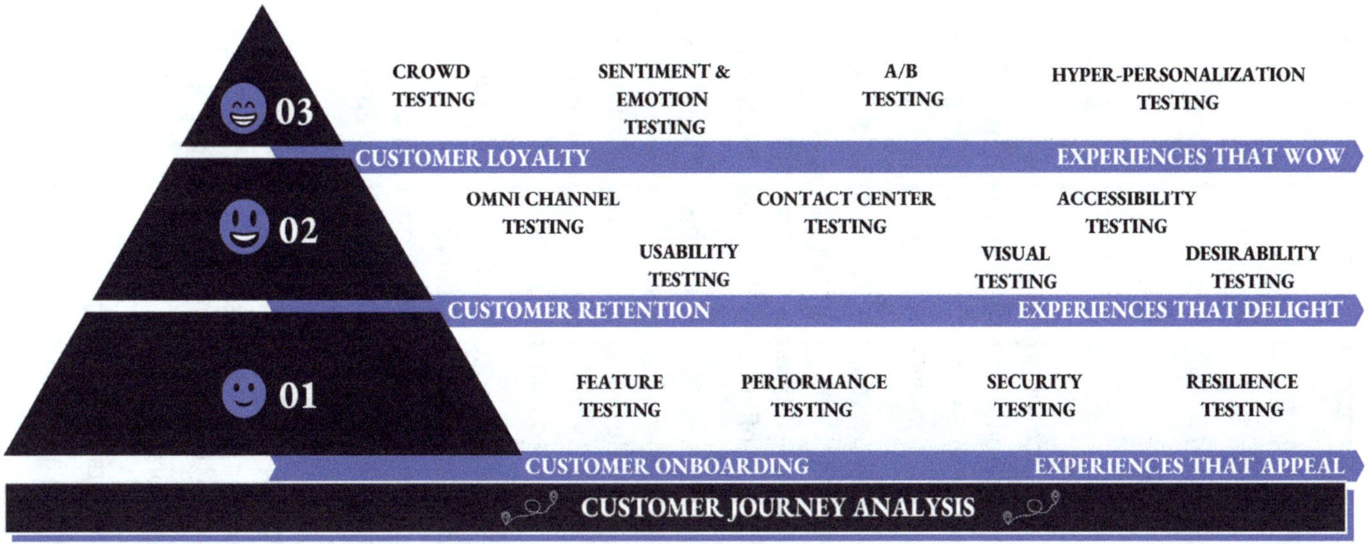

Experiences
that Appeal

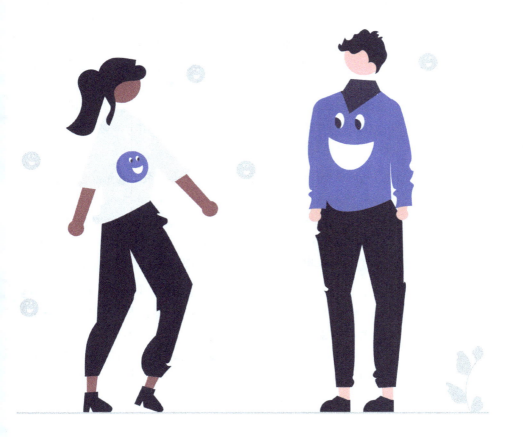

WHAT DO CUSTOMERS WANT?

For business executives throughout the world, it's the billion-dollar question: What do customers actually want?! Any company that can "crack the code" of the customer's mindset by predicting what users want and incorporating that into its product or service has a huge business differentiating advantage over its competition.

Unfortunately, users don't always know exactly what they want, and their buying decisions are not always based along rational lines. For one thing, according to research done by Ray Birdwhistell, 65 to 70% of human interactions are nonverbal.[4] Technology has fundamentally changed how humans interact, and accordingly we have developed a *new digital body language*. With the explosion of smart devices and our affinity for gadgets, nonverbal digital interactions by human beings will continue to rise. Every tap on your smartphone, every click on your mouse, every page you scroll through are forms of digital interaction. How can you use this digital body language to your advantage — i.e., to appeal to customers?

Another factor is our rational and emotional feedback loops. Customers may believe that they are thinking independently and making rational decisions when choosing to buy a product. In reality, however, its emotions, urges and the experience itself that play significant roles in our purchasing decisions.

At the same time, rational elements play a role too. Innovative marketing driven by a fancy website can pull a lot of traffic, but the final purchasing decision still will be based on factors such as trust, reputation, the right features, privacy, security, performance and accessibility. All these strands, rational and not, are integral parts of the customer experience. Often, appealing to a customer means having all the fundamentals in place.

---

4   http://www.culturalequity.org/alan-lomax/friends/birdwhistell

CHAPTER 1

FEATURES

"You've got to start with the customer experience and work back toward the technology - not the other way around." — Steve Jobs

- - - - - - - - - - - - - - - - -

The pandemic has ushered in an unprecedented disruption to the way business engages with the customer. According to Forrester's U.S. 2021 Customer Experience Index,[5] companies that revamped experiences excelled during the pandemic. And we have seen that customer-centric companies are today's most successful — Alphabet (Google), Meta (Facebook), Apple, Amazon, Netflix, etc.

But determining what exactly that experience should entail is not so simple. For example, a hugely important factor that influences a customer deciding on whether to buy a product or service is its *features*. After all, features define a product and differentiate it from similar products in the market. So, one could conclude that companies should just figure out which features their customers really want or need, and then provide these — and thus offer customers a superior experience. However, there is a tricky flip side to consider: Customers do not necessarily know what their needs are. It is impossible for them to say which features and experiences they like and want before they themselves experience the options.

---

5   https://www.forrester.com/press-newsroom/forresters-us-2021-customer-experience-index-shows-companies-that-revamped-experiences-excelled-during-the-pandemic/

Before the smartphone era, for example, customers had no "need" for a touchscreen, as they simply hadn't experienced it on a phone-like device to be able to decide if it is a useful feature or not. But when people started using it, they liked the experience and found it useful indeed. Thus it has become a seamless part of our daily lives. It's widely known that while Apple was not the first company to produce a smartphone, it created exceptional waves when it launched because the iPhone offered features that delivered unmatchable experience as compared to its competitors.

Similarly, when Apple launched its iPod there were already a number of good, well-made MP3 players in the market. But Apple was the only vendor to offer a true *platform* — its iStore's vast trove of music for sale meant users could *experience* music when they bought an iPod. And that made all the difference.

So customers in our digital world are really seeking experience, but features are how they get it. And nothing rankles a customer more than finding out the feature they paid for doesn't work — and consequently, that the experience is not satisfactory.

Clearly, in this digital space, quality engineers play a critical role to ensure that features and innovations work seamlessly to satisfy customer's experience needs. Because, again, a feature that doesn't work totally reliably is merely an overture — tantalizing the customer without delivering.

The Right Features

Some simple definitions: *Features* describe what a product can do, and *experience* describes the emotion of using those features. In digital, it is fair to say that *experience is the feature that always works*. And quality assurance is how to get there.

To get from customer wants to features, and from features to quality experience, a few basic questions need answering:

- *Who is the end user of the product?*
- *What are their needs?*
- *How does this feature benefit the customer?*
- *How can you ensure the features always work?*

Building the Right Features

Building the right features and *building features right* are two distinct things. Clearly, the first stage is determining the right features, which requires extensive collaboration and commitment within an organization. Some corporate cultures seem far better attuned to this pursuit than others, but even smooth-running, innovative companies can blunder at interpreting consumer culture.

How can you avert the next flop in your company (such as the infamous Ford Edsel)? First off, don't make the error — common in today's digital world — of focusing on innovation for its own sake while failing to align on what customers really need and want. These needs and wants drive customers' buying decisions, so companies that want to stay relevant are constantly on the lookout for features their customers want. Organizations use many methods to do so, including detailed customer surveys about what features they expect in your products. The feedback received could even be contradictory, so it is critical to make broader sense of the input and arrive at the right features. Sophisticated data analysis is essential here.

> *"Your most unhappy customers are your greatest source of learning."* — *Bill Gates*[6]

Other means of "listening to your customer" include interviews, online feedback, focus groups and social media. The greater mission is not just to identify customers' needs but to translate this knowledge into proper action — i.e., refining the features of the product.

---

6   *https://libquotes.com/bill-gates/works/business-@-the-speed-of-thought*

Building Features Right

Once your organization has a handle on what features to build, the next step is building them right. In this, choosing the right development and assurance strategies is key. There are three leading methodologies that help modern teams to ensure that desired features always work:

◆ *Building features for personas*
◆ *Behavior-driven development (BDD)*
◆ *Model-based testing (MBT)*

It is critical to have a good, clear understanding of these three approaches in order to strategize effectively.

Build Features for Personas

Customer-centricity is not natural for people. Our natural tendency is to be self-centered, which influences the products we develop and translates to product-centricity.[7] An effective way to counter our innate tendencies is by building features for *personas* — composite archetypes representing key traits of large segments of your customer base. Personas, which are derived from data collected via user research and web analytics, describe who your ideal customers are — what their days are like, the challenges they face, what they want, the decisions they make, goals, attitudes, etc.

An essential part of creating personas is making them as realistic and detailed as possible, which will best furnish the team with a tangible sense that they are building applications for the personas, in empathy with the customer base.

---

7   *Human Computer Interaction Handbook: Fundamentals, Evolving Technologies, and Emerging Applications by Julie A. Jacko*

Benefits of Personas

There are quite some benefits of using personas in your development processes. Below are key benefits of using personas from an experience perspective.

- **Personas define your customers**

Using personas helps your company define for whom you are creating your products, such as software applications, and why. With personas, development teams must consider which types of users are most critical to the business and ensure their requirements will be met. The biggest benefit is the mindset shift that occurs when developers adopt a persona-based perspective.

- **Personas define where your customers spend time**

What customers actually *do* within your app is crucial, since such behavior can help reveal problem areas that stymie users in using the app. Where they spend most of their time vs. what parts of the app get no attention is vital information for determining which features to implement and their order of priority.

- **Personas enhance empathy**

Empathy — the understanding of how other people think and feel — is a potent tool in app development. By mapping the emotions of your customers to one or more personas, it is possible to align these emotions with the features developed.

Behavior-Driven Development (BDD)

Another useful technique for building features aligned to customer needs is behavior analysis. The *behavior-driven development (BDD)* process for software arose out of frustrations with test-driven development (TDD). The TDD process entails writing automated acceptance tests before building the program code. After the program is written, the tests are immediately run against it to verify whether the program meets the criteria. Though TDD accelerated the development process by automating acceptance tests, it only served to automate teams' misunderstandings and ambiguities concerning requirements and desired functionality. This is where BDD came of age: to create a common understanding of the features and their intended uses.

In BDD, projects are delivered in sets of features. *Features essentially define the experience that a customer has with the product.*

One major misconception about BDD is that it is seen as a technical methodology that requires specific tooling and a particular programming language to work. Rather, BDD is primarily a conceptual approach that works for all technologies and project situations. Even though BDD sounds simple, embracing it across different roles remains a challenge. Company culture — the prevailing mindset — is perhaps the major reason for the underutilization of BDD. Change, however, is happening, as more teams adopt the Agile software development methodology to deliver projects.

BDD Methodology & Framework

The BDD framework comprises three stages: The *behavior stage,* where a ubiquitous language describes the behavior; the *glue code stage,* in which technical code interacts with the application; and the *reporting stage.* The behavior phase is usually written in the Gherkin language, but the glue code phase can be done with any programming language of choice.

Exhibit 2: Three stages of the BDD framework

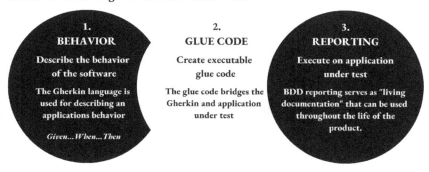

- *Behavior*

Gherkin is a human- and machine-readable language for describing an application's behavior under certain conditions. Its simple style of representing tests is a *given-when-then* format:

- **Given** *represents the precondition for the behavior.*
- **When** *represents the actual intended behavior.*
- **Then** *represents the expected result of the behavior.*

BDD emphasizes the importance of a domain-specific language that everyone can understand. Gherkin is the most popular and obvious choice for domain knowledge, as it brings structure to the description of behavior and is also readable by both humans and machines. Above all, it's popular as a format because it is how people speak naturally and is precise and succinct (in comparison with several pages of requirement documents).

- *Glue code*

The glue code bridges the Gherkin statements and the application under testing. In other words, it glues the behavior layer and the machine layer. Glue code can be written in any programming language of choice such as Java, JavaScript, Ruby, etc. However, a best practice is to write the glue code in the same language as the application's. As a rule, all functional aspects need to be handled at the behavior layer and all technical aspects — like setting up data, passing data to variables, etc. — should be handled by the glue code.

- *Report*

Reporting is an integral part of any framework, and BDD reports have some special uses unlike other frameworks. Other than the obvious role of providing execution status, BDD reporting serves as "living documentation" that can be used throughout the life of the product. This avoids any gap between specifications and what is actually realized.

For example, a business-to-business (B2B) company can forward these reports to its customers to highlight the quality checks that were already done on the product. This will avoid any overlaps, as well as giving customers the necessary confidence concerning quality. BDD scripts are also useful as user manuals to explain to end customers how features work.

Benefits of BDD

- *Breaks the communication barrier*

BDD is collaborative by design: Everyone in the team joins forces to create feature specifications. Since it is conducted in a language understandable by everyone, BDD breaks the communication gap and eliminates requirement leakages. BDD scenarios can act as descriptions for end users, requirements for product owners, acceptance criteria for developers, test cases for testers and automation scripts for automation specialists.

- *Executable requirements & acceptance*

With BDD, the focus is on customers' behavior, value and needs. While BDD as a methodology is independent of technology, it facilitates development efforts by defining acceptance criteria in a form that can be easily automated. Thus, BDD serves a dual purpose, acting as both specifications and automated acceptance tests.

BDD Anti-patterns & Solutions

- *BDD is not a tool*

Despite its popularity, BDD remains one of the most misunderstood methodologies in software development. One of the most common mistakes concerning BDD is that people treat it technically as a tool or as a set of automation scripts. Too frequently, testers or developers describe the behaviors without collaborating with other product stakeholders. Without collaboration, creating BDD statements is useless; it only adds an additional layer to your automation.

- *Writing scenarios*

As a visible side effect of treating BDD as a technical tool, the scenarios that are written to describe behaviors tend to be technical as well. It is sometimes difficult to avoid technical details, as the scenarios are executable test cases. However, describing a behavior with too many technical parameters and references can defeat the purpose of BDD, which advocates a ubiquitous language understood by all.

Another common anti-pattern in describing behaviors is writing scenarios with several steps, i.e., given-when-then *combinations*. The essence of the BDD approach is that each scenario specification should focus on only one individual behavior. Having several steps that combine multiple behaviors in one scenario can cause ambiguity, miscommunication and test gaps.

Model-Based Testing (MBT)

MBT is a technique in which test cases/scripts are generated from a model that describes the functionality of the application. MBT not only improves quality by increasing coverage, but also reduces development time by finding issues early.

Exhibit 3: Model based testing

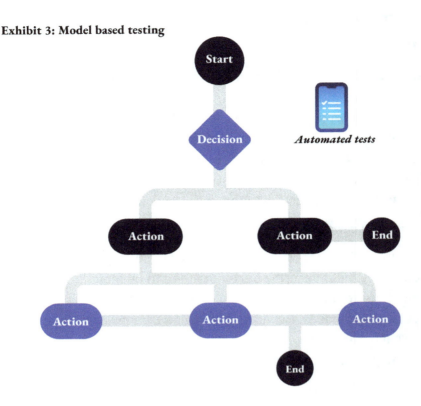

Requirements are modeled as process flows that visualize the functionality of the application, and these are then reviewed by the whole team. MBT tools ensure technical completeness of the model by confirming that all loops in the process flow are closed; i.e., every starting node has an ending node.

As in BDD, making a model that visualizes the functional aspects of the application triggers discussion among the three amigos: developers, testers and business. These conversations improve the quality of the model, thereby increasing the quality of the requirements.

An empirical case study conducted at the European Space Agency (ESA) on the effectiveness of MBT found that it resulted in significant reductions in test efforts. Under MBT, testing-related activities took only 1,135 hours compared to 3,735 hours for manual testing.[8]

MBT Process Steps

- **Building the model**

One of the most popular languages for modeling is the Unified Modeling Language (UML), which includes a set of graphic notations that can describe complicated behaviors of a system in a simplified manner. A wide range of model types can be used in MBT, such as process flow models, data flow models, control flow models, decision tables, etc.

The first step is to determine which functionality to model and in which order. One effective strategy is to model the critical and main flow first and then add details to build the sub flow. This is because it is important to keep models simple and readable. However, modeling a large application involves many process steps and flows, which would make the model extremely complex and thus unreadable. Building sub-models serves to maintain simplicity: So the main model will have the high-level flow, while sub models are designed for the details.

- **Generate test cases**

Once the model is built, the next step is to generate test cases. Test cases can cover all possible situations that may occur, but executing every scenario would consume a huge amount of time. So an optimization technique must be used to arrive at the best possible set of test cases. Several optimization methods can be used, individually or in combination, for this: decision pairs, step coverage or edge coverage.

---

8   https://www.researchgate.net/profile/Michael-Felderer/ publication/280948823_A_Case_Study_on_the_Efficiency_of_Model-Based_ Testing_at_the_European_Space_Agency/links/55ce4e1f08aee19936fc5a92/A-Case-Study-on-the-Efficiency-of-Model-Based-Testing-at-the-European-Space-Agency.pdf

- *Make test automation scripts*

The test cases generated are then transformed into concrete executable automated tests. Most MBT tools provide options to generate automated scripts based on the model. Usually, a separate abstraction layer is maintained in the model to create configurations for the automation scripts. This layered approach has the advantage of being independent of the language used for tests. With a configuration change, the tests can easily be used in other environments for or other applications.

- *Execute & analyze the results*

The executable test cases are then run against the system under test (SUT). Depending on the MBT tool chosen, execution can happen within the MBT tool environment itself or via existing tools and platforms. Finally, the test execution results are analyzed, and then corrective actions to fix the bugs are taken.

Advantages of MBT

MBT offers many advantages, such as a high degree of automation, the ability to generate high volumes of test cases and automatic impact analysis. It expands the statistical possibilities of software quality. Among the most significant advantages of MBT are the following. .

- *Shift left the quality assurance process*

MBT is a good way to validate requirements before models are built. Most often, software issues are introduced at the very beginning of the project, during the requirements phase. In an Agile team, requirements change rapidly and often, and it is very hard for teams to manually determine the impact of these changes. MBT can precisely point out the impact of change throughout downstream systems. It can also generate suitable tests specifically to check the impact of changes.

Shift left is all about bringing quality engineering upfront in the development process. Models can provide early feedback, revealing design flaws.

- **Increase in test coverage**

Models cover all permutations — every possible path, possibility and combination of events that can occur in a product. Since MBT also generates test cases automatically, they are generated for every occurrence and combination as well. Sometimes the models are more robust than the actual implementation.

- **Test case optimization**

If you are working on a complex mission-critical project, the number of test cases covering all possible combinations can be overwhelming. Deciding how much testing is enough and choosing the test cases to execute can be difficult because of the risks involved. MBT tools use algorithms to optimize and determine the test cases that need to be executed. This optimization can reduce the number of test cases up to 10% without compromising the coverage.

- **Usage-based test optimization**

In this technique, usage patterns of customers are analyzed and test cases on functions that matter most to the user are developed.

- **Reduce complexity & errors**

With manual testing, test quality is highly dependent on the test engineer, and the test design process is often based on the tester's experience level. With the use of the scientific approach and optimizing algorithms, human error and the number of test cases generated are controlled. The whole test design process is repeatable, which reduces complexity considerably.

- **Reduce excessive documentation**

Just as a picture is worth a thousand words, a visual representation of a SUT is far more vivid than a verbal description in a document.

People tend to skim over requirements that span pages and that can lead to mistakes in requirements interpretation. It helps in the Agile world as well, where requirements are split into small chunks and a holistic picture of the intended functionality is lost.

Limitations of MBT

- **One cannot assume that a formal (complete and consistent) model of the software system always exists.** There can be gaps between the actual requirements and the model, or between the model and how the system was actually built. Human error and incomplete requirements generally contribute to such discrepancies.
- **Modeling is hard.** Although at the outset modeling looks easy for everyone, in practice it requires specialized skills to do it right. Leading deterrents to proper modeling practice are the lack of holistic knowledge of the system plus a dearth of effective design principles.
- **Upfront investment is required to make the model.** A lot of research on how the system is meant to work and how it is actually implemented needs to be done — especially for existing products.

Though the challenges above can hinder companies starting to embrace MBT, the benefits to end customers far outweigh the initial hurdles. Keys to a successful MBT implementation are to introduce the methodology in smaller pilots, train the team and use proper tools.

CHAPTER 2

PRIVACY

"A business cares more than anything else about its bottom line, so if privacy helps its bottom line, it will consider privacy a priority." — Paul Bernal, Univ. of East Anglia Law Lecturer[9]

Now that customer data is the lifeblood for every business, a commitment to keep the data safe, secure and private is essential for companies to survive in the digital economy. Though some organizations realize this need, data privacy is still an afterthought for many. And so issues involving data security — at both private and public organizations — erupt regularly in the news.[10]

Privacy and compliance have always played a secondary role as companies spend most of their time and effort on building new features — including the personalized services customers require to remain competitive. Such personalization is based on reams of personal data — information that today's customers seem happy to provide if it will improve their digital experience and they have confidence their data will be used sensibly.

So these competing drives — providing personalized services and maintaining data privacy — seem to be at odds with each other. Which do customers want more? Answer: Both! Everyone wants convenience

---

9   https://www.theguardian.com/media-network/2015/jul/23/privacy-becomes-a-priority-for-businesses-and-their-consumers
10   https://www.securitymagazine.com/articles/96667-the-top-data-breaches-of-2021

and privacy. Companies must realize that oft-ignored dimensions of privacy and security are foundation blocks on which digital companies build their capabilities.

This leaves us with the big question this chapter tackles: How can companies provide enhanced customer experience while safeguarding privacy?

Privacy vs. Personalization

Personalization means individualizing products and services to a particular customer, sometimes through offers, product recommendations and other content, based on their previous actions, preferences, demographics and other personal data. The more information you have about the customer, the more you can personalize.

Personalization is not a new concept. Retailers have tried to provide personalized customer experiences throughout history.

> 😊 Short Bytes
>
> For example, in days of yore, it was difficult for hatmakers to measure the circumference and precise contours of customers' heads. Standard sizes were the norm until the mid-1800s when Lock & Co. (the world's oldest hatmaker) adopted the Conformateur[11] — a head-measuring device invented in France by Allié-Maillard. Lock & Co. still uses the device for customized hats.

But can we provide this customized personal experience for everyone in the digital world?

Everyone knows the example of Amazon, which offers users an expanse of customized recommendations on its landing pages, based on their previous search, browsing and buying behaviors. According to

---

11   https://www.lockhatters.com/pages/history

Business Insider, though such personalization may not be accurate every time, companies that have implemented the approach have seen sales increase by 6–10%.[12]

Indeed, customers' expectations of receiving these personalized recommendations are high. This push, driven by advancements in analytics and AI-derived insights, has changed the very nature of the online customer experience dramatically, and is having an impact in other sectors as well.

But along with companies' ability to analyze and extract patterns from data comes a responsibility to handle it with care. Aware of the data breaches and misuses of personal data they face, and the potential that their information will be used inappropriately, customers are rightly concerned. Pressure has been building internationally for increased legislation to address new forms of data misuse, and for stricter rules on using customer data for any purpose other than its intended one. The most significant new data-protection legislation to arise so far is the European Union's General Data Protection Regulation (GDPR). The GDPR clarifies what data is being stored and for what purpose, which is fundamental in balancing privacy and personalization. Europe is also building on the GDPR intiative to cover AI (see next section for more insight).[13]

12   https://www.businessinsider.com/personalization-may-be-the-key-to-competing-with-amazon-2017-11?international=true&r=US&IR=T
13   https://www.lexology.com/library/detail.aspx?g=e1c63803-a8e2-4479-85ff-c4d7b5d2931a

The European Union's Data Protection Agencies (DPAs) received more than 95,000 complaints from EU citizens since the enforcement of the General Data Protection Regulation in May 2018. Out of the complaints received, 65,000 of them were data breach notifications.[14]

The above is the wider context for a more specific question pertaining to IT professionals: *Should you use customer data for IT software development and the validation process?*

Though no legislation answers this question directly, there is widespread consensus among experts that it is quite dangerous to do so. Making customer data available to a larger group of people on less secure environments increases the chance of a data breach, which can be disastrous if it leads to reputation loss or triggers huge penalties for failure to take sufficient compliance measures.

In reality, it is still a widespread practice to use actual customer data for IT development processes, especially for testing. The rationale behind is that it is highly challenging to simulate all real-world customer data combinations and scenarios.

However, in this brave new age of AI, that limitation no longer applies. Ultimately, companies can still provide the personalized customer experience while being compliant (which we will explore in Chapter 9).

---

14   http://www.europarl.europa.eu/meetdocs/2014_2019/plmrep/
COMMITTEES/LIBE/DV/2019/02-25/9_EDPB_report_EN.pdf

The biggest data breach in history took place at Yahoo in 2013 when more than three billion accounts were compromised. The compromised data included users' names, birth dates, phone numbers and passwords.[15]

Privacy in the Age of AI

AI is bound to affect humanity in both positive and negative ways, especially as it impacts privacy. We are only just embarking on the AI journey which is set to cause huge repercussions to our society. As yet, there are no regulatory laws or regulations specifically to protect data processed by an AI-driven system. The problem with AI is that it is impossible to define the purpose of the data collected or to predict how the algorithms — which can seem to have a "mind of their own" — will interpret it. Already, we have seen numerous examples where AI systems have applied racial or gender biases.[16]

We see two primary ways in which AI is poised to affect privacy:

- **Profiling**

An increasing number of AI systems have been developed for questionable uses such as scoring, classifying, evaluating and ranking people — most often, without the consent of the individuals involved. China's Social Credit System is a prime example of profiling people with AI using multiple data points. China's system will monitor the behavior of citizens and assign ranks based on the data. As foreseen, the system will punish badly behaved citizens by denying certain services.

Profiling has beneficial uses, such as in law enforcement where arrested people are assessed as flight risks in the bail-setting process,

---

15   https://www.secureworld.io/industry-news/top-10-data-breaches-of-all-time
16   https://time.com/5520558/artificial-intelligence-racial-gender-bias/

or potential crime victims are identified so they can be alerted. But the problem with this technology is that no AI system is foolproof — i.e., without biases and 100% accurate. Perhaps the best depiction of this technology taken to an extreme was the 2002 film *Minority Report*, in which the "precrime" department arrests murderers before they commit the crime.

- **Facial recognition**

Facial recognition, a biometric technology that can identify individuals based on digital images or video frames, is still young and deployed widely. Depending on how it is used, it can pose a real threat to individual privacy. However, it can be used to save lives too, such as by identifying security threats at airports. The "devil is in the details" of its deployment, but its potential for misidentification of suspects and racial discrimination should not be underestimated. The big problem, from a societal standpoint, is in not getting an individual's consent to track them.

Data is the fuel of AI; data helps AI systems learn continuously and make intelligent decisions. *The only way to control AI systems is to control the data used for training them.* On the other hand, too many restrictions imposed will make AI evolution impossible. As noted above, ensuring the right privacy at each step of AI application development and starting to govern AI with well-conceived laws are the only ways to avoid future catastrophe.

How to Ensure Privacy

Ensuring privacy requires that a company establishes proper policies based on clearly defined principles that clarify who can access customer data and for what purposes. Putting policies in place is just the first step. Quite often, enforcing these policies gets sidetracked as a low priority behind other more pressing CIO tasks. As data protection laws become stricter and fines heavier, companies must realize that enforcing these policies could make or break their reputation. Further, broadcasting these policies so they are transparent and visible for everyone would help boost customer confidence.

There are three approaches which are all necessary to ensure privacy in your organization:

- ◆ *Privacy by default*
- ◆ *Privacy by design*
- ◆ *Use of synthetic data*

Privacy by Default

Privacy by default means when a product or service is released to the public, the strictest privacy settings should apply by default without any manual input from the end user. One widely known example is the opt-out setting instead of an opt-in. For example, nobody receives newsletter or promotions by default, but rather they must explicitly subscribe.

There are three essential elements that together constitute privacy by default.

Minimal Data Collection

This principle, a virtual golden rule, is to minimize the risk of data breach by collecting only the bare minimum of data required to provide the intended service.

Indeed, many users are wary of providing their consent to store sensitive financial information like credit card details, especially when they do not know the organization well. Before you decide what information to collect from your customer, detailed research is usually required. Also remember that long forms that ask for unnecessary information could turn users away from submitting and completing an order.

Exhibit 4: Examples of customer data sources

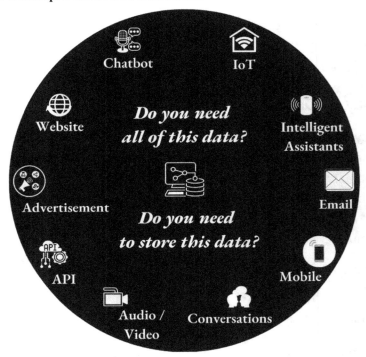

Retention & Portability

This principle is to retain personal information only as long as necessary to fulfil the original purpose of its collection. So, for example, when customers leave the company, remove personally identifiable information collected from them as well. Many companies are paranoid about deleting data from their live systems, owing partly to poor design and partly to a lack of knowledge about data flows and dependencies. Legislation such as GDPR not only imposes a mechanism to delete data but also defines strict retention periods for storing personal information.

Data portability is the ability to move data among applications, services or customers. Customers should have the luxury of moving their personal data from one service provider to another. Though the law enforces this right, consensus among companies on what data formats and standards to follow is still taking shape. The practical implementation of complete data portability remains a challenge.

Transparency & Purpose of Use

Do you ever read the terms and conditions fully before signing up for a service? You are not alone. It is a proven fact that very few people read the terms and conditions properly before agreeing by clicking. Most of these documents are far too long and tedious, and many companies use them merely to cover themselves legally instead of informing the customers what they are signing on for.

Digital companies face the challenge of devising innovative ways to make their policies transparent and lucid to customers. We need to build several interactive controls within products to help customers clearly understand how their data will be stored, shared and used, without damaging the customer experience.

Though it is common practice for companies to use personal data for analytical, product development and testing purposes, few companies have explicit consent from their customers to do so. Making the process transparent by informing customers about the exact use of their data is the best path to trust-building.

Privacy by Design

A "design-thinking" perspective should permeate our approach to business and technology innovation, to the customer experience — and to privacy as well. *Privacy by design* embeds privacy in every design decision from the beginning. It anticipates and prevents privacy violations. Here are the most commonly used design principles.

Ensure Proper Access Rights

Access control regulates "who or what" can view resources in a given environment. When it comes to privacy, clear establishment of rules on who has access to customer data and for what purpose is a necessity.

Traditionally, companies use role based access control (RBAC) where specific roles such as support and operational engineers are privileged to access production systems. But sadly, many companies struggle with access control. According to Varonis's 2021 data risk report, nearly two-thirds of companies have 1,000+ sensitive files open to every employee.[17] It is high time for digital companies to reassess historic access role assignments within the organization. With human error accounting for a whopping 85% of enterprise data breaches,[18] ensuring proper access rights is a critical part of privacy by design.

Pseudo-anonymization & Obfuscation of Data

Obfuscation is making something less clear, less legible or harder to understand. Data obfuscation is also popularly referred as anonymization, or masking; the terms are used interchangeably. By anonymizing data, companies can expose it as needed to test teams or database administrators without compromising compliance.

Implementing data obfuscation across the company involves five steps (see Exhibit 5).

---

17   https://info.varonis.com/hubfs/docs/research_reports/2021-Financial-Data-Risk-Report.pdf

18   https://www.tessian.com/research/the-psychology-of-human-error/

Exhibit 5: Data obfuscation steps

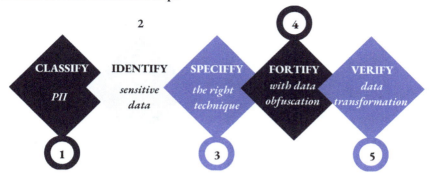

Classify

The first step toward compliant data management is to define and classify what constitutes personally identifiable information (PII) for your organization — i.e., which information or parts of information identify an individual? *What is your definition of PII?*

According to the Data Breach Report 2021,[19] customer PII is the most expensive and most common type of record lost in 44% of the breaches. The data that we voluntarily give up online while ordering products or registering for services (name, phone number, data of birth, etc.) can be a real threat in the wrong hands. In addition to the commonly identified personal information, some industry-specific information can be sensitive and traceable back to a person. For example, the internet protocol (IP) address is considered personal data as defined under EU laws.

Also consider that certain data items when looked at individually might not be sensitive but when combined with other data fields can be sensitive and can reveal a person's identity. In general, PII can be classified under two broad categories:

---

19   *https://www.ibm.com/downloads/cas/OJDVQGRY*

- *Direct PII*

Information that is unique to a person and can be used to directly identify that person is considered direct PII. Examples include passport and Social Security numbers.

- *Indirect PII*

Sensitive information that can be used in combination with one or more other pieces of information to identify a person can be grouped as indirect PII. For example, private information like date of birth by itself is not enough to identify a person, but combining it with a last name would probably be enough to do so. Data items like first names, DOB, gender, etc. could all be grouped as indirect PII.

Identify Sensitive Data

Once PII is clearly defined and the different types are established, the next step is to use this list to map where personal information is spread across the organization. The checklist can be used to locate all sensitive fields across the application databases.

Modern anonymization tools help with automatic discovery of PII, at least from databases. But no approach is foolproof and constant effort is required to ensure correct PII data discovery. One common approach is the use of regular genetic expression patterns to search the different sources for PII information.

Specify

After identifying PII data fields, the right anonymization technique needs to be chosen for each data item. The technique would depend on the data type, business requirements and the need to maintain integrity across databases. Sometimes a combination of anonymization techniques can be used to better protect the data.

- *Data encryption*

Data encryption translates data into a random key or meaningless text, such as ciphertext. Decryption is possible only by using the key that was used to encrypt the data.

The use of encryption goes back to the Roman Empire. The Roman army to encrypt military and other official messages used the *Caeser Shift Cipher*. In a shift cipher, each letter of the alphabet is shifted a certain number of places further down the alphabet. The number of places shifted is the key. In the Caesar Cipher, the key is three: A is replaced with D, B is replaced with E and so on. It worked back then, as most of Rome's enemies were illiterate at that time. Today's encryption methods of course are extremely advanced and difficult to decrypt.

Though encryption is one of the best methods to obfuscate data, it is not useful from a test data perspective as it reduces the quality of data rendering and adds overhead due to costly compute cycles.

- *Substitution*

Substitution is one of the best techniques from a test data quality perspective as it mimics the look and feel of real data without compromising its quality. Sensitive data is simply replaced by a dummy look-up value. Creating a proper look-up table with the right mix of data is the key in this technique.

For example, you can create a look-up table with names and addresses for the country your business is operating in. This will provide enough representation of data and will take care of details such as diacritics in names and proper addresses. This method maintains test data quality without compromising compliance.

- *Shuffling*

Shuffling means to simply move the data randomly within the column or columns. For example, shuffling individual values in a salary column would make it impossible for anyone to guess what an individual employee earns without changing the aggregate or average.

Though this is a common randomization technique, care should be taken that the new shuffled value is not the same as the original value. One could argue that this technique is not the best way to anonymize all types of data items, because even after shuffling, the sensitive data resides within the database. You can still obtain the list of all a company's customers, for instance, even though the data is not in a specific order.

- *Variance*

Variance is usually used to anonymize numeric fields such as payment amounts, salaries, etc. In this technique, a random variance percentage is added or subtracted from the original value. In some cases, however, even if all other details are anonymized, you should still be able to identify the transaction details of a particular person. For example, in an HR database, the person with the highest salary is generally one of the C-level executives at the company.

- *Nulling*

Nulling is a simple technique where sensitive information is deleted from the database. It is sometimes easier to delete data than to use complex algorithms, but one must be careful to not reduce test data quality and consistency.

- *Translation*

With this technique, sensitive values are translated using specific mapping. For example, rules can be defined such that all instances of "A" get translated to "W" and all "1"s get translated to "7"s, etc. This works as a quick and efficient technique as long as the translation logic is not revealed or traced by users of the data.

Fortify

Execution of scripts happens after the mapping of the anonymization techniques.

- *In-place anonymization*

Companies that require the use of production data for development and quality assurance typically use in-place masking. Production data is first copied to a staging environment with secure access controls and then anonymization scripts are executed to create a "golden copy" which is then copied either in full volumes or subsets for analytics and testing purposes. Though this method does not drain the production environment on performance, storage requirements are higher to maintain the golden copy database.

- *In-flight masking*

In-flight masking is used if you choose not to store sensitive customer data anywhere else other than on production systems, even temporarily. In this type of masking, sensitive data is transformed while being copied to other environments from production. This reduces the need to have any additional storage for anonymization purposes.

However, bear in mind that this process can cause severe performance drain on the production systems. This it is advisable to use in-flight anonymization when the production systems are not live to reduce any possible impact, especially on larger databases. Another disadvantage of this method is that the transformation rules specified for anonymization should have been proven already, before this technique is applied. It is inefficient to develop and test transformation rules while data is being copied.

Verify

After anonymization, the next step is to verify that all the intended fields have been transformed. It is also essential to check data integrity within and among databases and the impact on downstream systems.

Compiling audit trails and statistics before and after anonymization can help in the verification process.

Synthetic Data

Synthetic data is information that is *artificially generated* rather than collected from real-world situations. Using synthetic data for software testing purposes has its own merits. Though production data provides an accurate view of all customer scenarios, it only represents the current state. From a quality perspective, it is not sufficient, as it is important to test all the edge cases, negative scenarios and future data states. This makes test data generation an essential part of the software development process. Using generated data entirely for testing and analytics purposes reduces the risk of data breach and improves quality.

Though this is one of the most compliant methods, it can be a big step for organizations, which depend on live data to reduce dependencies and to generate all possible combinations of data. Quite often, it is the lack of knowledge on what to create that is the biggest hurdle in this approach.

Data can be generated in several ways, including the following:

- *Manual creation of data*

The *manual creation of data*, either through the application's GUI or directly into the database, is a common practice for testers creating data. For most of the edge cases, this method has value in the fact that customized data can be generated based on the test case. It is thus ideal for creating exotic test data where the objective is to test the application by brute force. However, it is time-consuming to create data manually, and so it leads to low productivity.

- *Data creation through test automation scripts*

One of the best ways to create data is by using *test automation scripts*. An ideal sequence would be to create data required for the automation scripts, run the tests and clean up the data after execution. This is a repeatable process and it can be scaled to create large volumes of data. The approach serves dual purposes: one can verify the automation scripts and generate data at the same time.

One best practice in this approach is to use APIs for automatic generation of data. API tests are usually more stable than GUI tests and the creation process is much quicker.

- *Data generation using specialized tools*

A commercial-off-the-shelf (COTS) package or an in-house tool can be used to directly inject data in the database. This is the fastest way of generating data and is ideal for generating large volumes of data, especially for performance testing purposes.

Though this approach is practical, do not get carried away by thinking a tool can solve all the test data problems. The fundamental problems of what to generate and when to generate would still remain in this approach.

- *Data creation using machine learning algorithms*

One huge advantage of machine learning algorithms is their ability to process huge amounts of data with ease and derive patterns and distributions of data. Knowing what to generate is the biggest challenge in the traditional data generation process. Often, even with sophisticated data generation techniques, it is difficult to generate data that represents the production environment with the right distribution and variety of data.

Machine learning algorithms can bridge this gap. By analyzing data distribution and data patterns in the production environment, it can then generate data with the exact distribution and pattern of data.

Exhibit 6: Data pattern analysis with machine learning

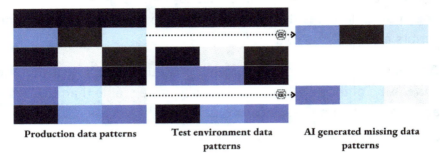

| Production data patterns | Test environment data patterns | AI generated missing data patterns |

Generative Adversarial Networks (GANs)

A *generative adversarial network (GAN)* is a type of machine learning algorithm composed of two neural networks: a generative network and a discriminative network. One part of the algorithm, called the *generator,* produces new instances of data and the discriminator classifies and validates data. GANs can mimic any distribution of data and can be extremely useful in generating data that exactly represents production data in terms of quality and distribution.

Exhibit 7: Generative adversarial networks

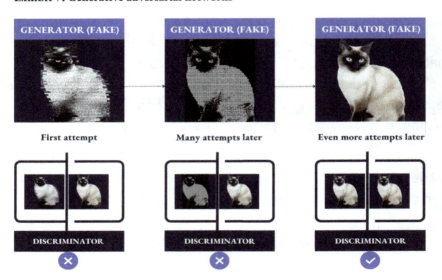

CHAPTER 3

SECURITY

"It takes 20 years to build a reputation and few minutes of cyber-incident to ruin it." — Stéphane Nappo, Global Chief Information Security Officer, Société Générale International Banking

----

Like privacy, security is absolutely essential for a satisfying user experience, and customers who encounter any security failure are likely to quickly become ex-customers. As customers' expectations for customer experience rise ever higher, their tolerance for glitches remains low. But good security breeds trust and loyalty. Unfortunately, many organizations still treat the security component as an afterthought or even an inhibitor to continuous development. For example, a recent survey of 350 IT decision-makers showed that half of DevOps teams still haven't incorporated app security into their continuous integration and development workflows.[20]

Bob Thomas (with follow-up development by Ray Tomlinson) in 1971 created the Creeper Worm— the world's first piece of malware. Although it did not carry out any malicious attack, it bounced between computers displaying the message, *"I'M THE CREEPER; CATCH ME IF YOU CAN."*[21] To us in the modern world, it looks quaint. Since this incident occurred, data breaches, cyberthreats, website hacking and data/identity theft have grown into terrible menaces that prey

---

20   https://www.synopsys.com/blogs/software-security/new-study-finds-security-in-devops-is-lagging/
21   https://en.wikipedia.org/wiki/Creeper_(program)

upon technology's advancement. Not surprisingly, one estimate pegs worldwide spending on cybersecurity reaching $133.7 billion in 2022.[22]

With our digital society so vulnerable to cyberattacks, the solution — *cybersecurity* — has a vast impact and influence. Cybersecurity is the practice of protecting systems, networks and programs from digital attacks. The consequences — both financial and reputational — of organizations not having sufficient cybersecurity are potentially huge, with impacts ranging from private homes to the entire nation or world.

Balancing Security & Experience

With over two billion people surfing the internet at any moment, how many of these users are aware of defensive cybersecurity? And how many of the sites which they access have rigorous security measures in place? The point: There are vast opportunities for hackers and spammers to launch malicious attacks.

However, the flip side is that too many security measures and authentications can damage customer experience by creating delays or other usability hassles. In fact, our human nature is to cut corners, for example by using a standard password across multiple accounts, services and devices. From an experience perspective, one just has to remember the password once. Nobody can remember all their passwords if they use a unique one for each account, especially if it has to be random and long.

In fact, however, reusing the same password across accounts and websites is one of the biggest IT risks that we expose ourselves to on a regular basis.

The question remains: How do we strike the right balance between customer experience and security? Are they a zero sum game where the more you have one, the less you have of another? In light of the fact that security breaches represent the gravest affronts to customer

---

22   https://legaljobs.io/blog/cyber-crime-statistics/

experience, the definition of CX must include the security dimension, and providing assurance of security is vital for positive customer experience. The IT goal: making all security processes as streamlined, transparent and painless as possible.

Authentication

Customers' online journey begins with authentication. As the saying goes, "First impression is the best impression," and so the speed, efficiency and security of the authentication leave a profound impact on the customer.

A "prime" example of an elevated authentication experience is the Amazon website. Amazon recognizes visitors the moment they enter the site from previous login history, and provides personalized shopping recommendations and other relevant options. Only when it is obviously required during checkout and payment, Amazon asks for the user's login credentials. So casual browsers, who just want to just look at a few products or run price comparisons, are not hindered by authentication protocols.

- *Step-up authentication*

Here, the security vs. CX balance depends partly on the exact actions the customer wishes to take, for which the authentication measure is calibrated. For instance, mobile banking app users' most frequent activity is to check account balances and view transactions. This would not require the same level of authentication as making a money transfer, for example. A simple, handy authentication mechanism like entering a pattern or code could be applied to let the customer use the app, and security can be stepped up incrementally when required. This balances the experience without compromising security.

- *Multifactor authentication (MFA)*

MFA is a security system that requires more than one method of authentication from independent categories of credentials to verify the user's identity. Such a system combines two or more independent factors, such as *what the user knows?* (password); *what the user has received?* (SMS token); and *who the user is?* (biometric information).

MFA is immensely secure, but forcing customers through multiple checks on their journey will soon induce frustration and premature departure. Unfortunately, most implementations of MFA lack proper understanding of the needs of the customer.

The best way to deploy MFA is via a risk-based approach, wherein login requests are scored based on parameters like a user's role, location, device settings and past history. When flagged, these parameters can trigger additional authentication mechanisms on a case-by-case basis. This substantially reduces the hardship for the customer while maintaining the required security levels.

- ***Knowledge-based authentication (KBA)***

KBA is a security measure that authenticates end users by asking them to answer specific "secret" security questions. With the emergence of IoT and connected devices, a short personal authentication question is the most convenient for customers. Some common ones: *What is the name of your first school? What is the name of your favorite pet? What is your mother's middle name? What was the first car you bought?*

While leading companies used KBA successfully in the past, it has become easy prey for modern hackers. Much of this information asked for by KBA is readily available on social media platforms and other places online, making it far too easy for cybercriminals to hack accounts. Thus, many companies are already phasing out KBA in favor of stronger tactics.

How to Secure CX

Did you bother to change the default password of the fancy little gadget that you bought recently? Research and experience reveal that most people don't even take that basic precautionary step. Several years back, a Russian website indexed over 73,000 locations with unsecured security cameras in 256 countries.[23] They could do so because most the camera buyers were using default usernames and passwords even though the manual strongly recommended that passwords be changed immediately post installation. The security problem soon will be drastically intensified as IoT is poised to usher in the next big home technology revolution after the proliferation of smartphones. (See Chapter 6 for a deep dive into IoT.) IoT comprises billions of connected devices, collecting and sharing data — all of it potentially hackable. The technology industry has historically acted on security issues only after a major incident makes the vulnerability apparent. With IoT, the problem is clear right from day one.

When it comes to security, your product is only as good as the latest cybercrime breach it prevents. Every day, new malware is created in the world, and we don't have enough cybersecurity professionals to combat it. (There is a worldwide shortage of about three million of such experts.[24]) Organizations now require effective means to identify and protect against imminent cyberthreats.

These three measures need to be in place to ensure a secure customer experience:

- *Winning customer trust*
- *Security by design*
- *Application security testing*

Winning Customer Trust

Trust is the glue that bonds a customer to a brand. It is not a spontaneous response, but something that develops over time. Earning customer trust involves establishing it, nurturing it and even sometimes restoring it in times of turmoil.

23   https://www.hackread.com/website-streams-from-private-security-cameras/
24   https://www.forbes.com/sites/forbestechcouncil/2021/03/26/
do-you-have-a-cybersecurity-talent-shortage-dont-require-a-four-year-
degree/?sh=5ecc27ef1b88

Establish Trust

Any customer using your product obviously wants to know it is safe. With the growing number of phishing incidents and online scams, customers are understandably cautious and looking for visible signs to ensure the site they are using is safe. In web-based applications, for example, customers generally perceive websites with the green-lock to be safer. The lock means traffic to and from the website is encrypted, which gives users a sense of security.

- *Vulnerability disclosure policy*

A *vulnerability disclosure policy* provides clear guidelines to ethical hackers or anyone who stumbles across a vulnerability to report it to the appropriate person or channel. Yet, according to a hacker report in 2018,[25] nearly one in four hackers hadn't reported a discovered vulnerability because the company did not have a channel in which to disclose it. In addition to providing the right channels, companies must assure customers and finders that no legal action will be initiated if the vulnerabilities were found in good faith or by accidental violations. Companies such as Google, Facebook and Microsoft encourage reporting bugs and other vulnerabilities through "Bug Bounty" programs in which the reporter receives monetary compensation, recognition or even job offers.

Maintain Trust

To reinforce a trusted brand, listen to your customers and engage with them to provide periodic warnings on threats, plus regular sharing of updates on security policies and compliance requirements will maintain trust. Trust is a moving target like any other strategic business goal. To build lasting customer relationships, organizations must understand that trust is a dynamic pursuit that requires agility and constant evaluation.

---

25   https://www.hackerone.com/sites/default/files/2018-01/2018_Hacker_Report_0.pdf

Restore Trust

No matter how fortified a company's security walls are, damaging security breaches can occur — and severely damage a company's reputation. While lessons are continually being learned by security experts, hackers are becoming more sophisticated and innovative – as a result of rapid technological advancements. *How does a company emerge from a security crisis and restore trust with its customers?*

- **Transparency & communication**

First off, to regain trust with your customers, you must tell and show them that you are in control of the situation. Take ownership, apologize and reach out to the customers directly. It is far better for the customers to learn about the breach from you rather than to hear it in the media.

- **Response plan**

A security breach response plan is a defined set of actions that help organizations detect and respond to incidents in a fast, coordinated manner. This is an area that needs improvement widely. According to a study from IBM, 77% of business leaders did not have a formal "cybersecurity incident plan" applied consistently across their organizations.[26] Firing a scapegoat is not enough. Customers need to see visible improvement in policies and security to regain their trust.

Security by Design

Security by design is an approach to software (and even hardware) development that seeks to minimize systems' vulnerabilities and reduce the attack surface through designing and building security — and testing — in every phase of the software development lifecycle (SDLC). It sounds very sensible, so one would think many companies have adopted this approach already. In reality, however, security by

---

26   *https://newsroom.ibm.com/2018-03-14-IBM-Study-Responding-to-Cybersecurity-Incidents-Still-a-Major-Challenge-for-Businesses*

design is still at its infancy. There is large room for progress, but at least most mature development teams already employ the DevSecOps model, which incorporates more frequent security scans and early flaw fixes.[27] Integrating security in the design phase requires *doing a proper threat analysis and involving customers in the security engineering process.*

> ☺ Short Bytes
>
> *On Dec. 9, 2021, security researchers discovered a flaw in the code of Log4j, a java software library used for logging in applications worldwide. This flaw was estimated to be present in over 100 million instances globally and the resulting vulnerability was rated 10/10 on the Common Vulnerability Scoring System. The risk has caused waves of panic across both private and public sector industries alike, with critical systems like Apple iCloud, ElasticSearch, AWS, Twitter and even Minecraft exposed.[28]*

Threat Analysis: Know Your Enemies

Threats are anything that can go wrong or attack your information assets. Creating a threat profile is the first step in defining what security tests are required. Such a profile includes information about critical assets, threat actors and threat scenarios. Some of the more common digital threats are as follows.

▪ *Privilege elevation*

Privilege elevation is a type of network intrusion that takes advantage of programming errors or design flaws to grant the attacker elevated access to the network and its associated data and applications.

---

27   https://digitally.cognizant.com/how-devsecops-can-help-plug-a-6-trillion-drain-codex4797
28   https://www.cisecurity.org/log4j-zero-day-vulnerability-response

- **SQL injection**

SQL injection is the most common application-layer attack technique in which malicious SQL statements are inserted into an entry field for execution. SQL injection is a grave threat as it can get critical information from the server database.

- **Denial of service**

A *denial-of-service* attack is one meant to make a machine or network resource unavailable to its intended users by temporarily or indefinitely disrupting services of a host connected to the internet.

- **Botnet**

A *botnet* is a collection of compromised internet-connected devices, each of which running one or more bots. The owners of the individual PCs may not even know that they are being used for running malicious programs.

Botnets first entered public awareness in early 2000, when a Canadian teenager launched a series of distributed denial-of-service (DDoS) attacks against several high-profile websites.[29] Cybercriminals use botnets to mine cryptocurrencies such as Bitcoin.

- **Cross-site scripting (XSS)**

XSS is a client-side code injection in which the attacker injects malicious scripts into web pages belonging to legitimate websites. According to recent statistics, XSS is still the top "high-risk" application security issue, with a 37.2% occurrence rate.[30]

- **URL manipulation**

URL manipulation, also called URL rewriting, is the process of altering the parameters in a URL to redirect to third-party sites, load sensitive files off the server, and so on.

---

29   *https://www.itworldcanada.com/article/canadian-teen-arrested-in-ddos-web-attacks/34161*
30   *https://info.edgescan.com/hubfs/Edgescan2021StatsReport.pdf*

- **Data manipulation**

Data manipulation is the practice of altering digital documents and other information in ways that are disastrous for corporations or individuals, or provide misleading results on research. With AI and machine learning so heavily reliant on data, new attack surfaces for data manipulation are being exposed. AI-driven technologies are poised to make critical decisions in the fields of healthcare, finance, education, etc., so manipulating data can lead to far-reaching negative consequences.

- **Identity spoofing**

Identity spoofing is a technique in which the credentials of a legitimate user or a device are used to launch attacks against network hosts, steal data or bypass access control.

- **Password cracking**

Password cracking is a process of recovering passwords from data storage or through data transmitted by a computer system. Password cracking employs a number of techniques to achieve this goal, like generating passwords through brute force, using algorithms to crack passwords, spidering, etc.

> 😊 Short Bytes
>
> *Do you know that world password day is celebrated every year on the first Thursday of May? Intel[31] created the day to stress the importance of protecting ourselves via strong passwords. According to a 2021 study from NordPass covering 50 countries, "123456" remains the most popular password for the second year running.[32]*

---

31   https://community.intel.com/t5/Blogs/Thought-Leadership/Big-Ideas/
Celebrating-the-8th-Annual-World-Password-Day/post/1335057
32   https://nordpass.com/most-common-passwords-list

Involving Customers in Security Engineering

Security by design is not just for new applications. There are billions of lines of vulnerable code already in the market, waiting to be exploited by a hacker. Taking care of your existing applications, which were not necessarily built with security in mind, is another core principle of security by design.

Security violations often involve customer accounts and identity, making customers wary of sharing personal details and sensitive financial information such as credit card numbers on sites they do not trust. The best way to put a worried customer at ease is to both inform and engage them: Involve them in the security process by requiring strong passwords, additional authentication or even biometric information such as fingerprints or iris scans.

- *Feedback & recognition*

The key to involving customers is to actively encourage them to provide timely feedback whenever they notice a possible security flaw or breach. Some companies reward citizens who report a security flaw in their product to encourage more people actively looking for vulnerabilities. For example, as mentioned above, *bug bounties* are the rewards offered by many websites, organizations and companies for reporting glitches, especially security exploits and vulnerabilities. The Department of Defense under Barack Obama's Administration ran the "Hack the Pentagon" program in 2016. Two hundred and fifty hackers participated, resulting in 138 legitimate vulnerabilities eligible for the bounty. Though $150,000 was paid in bounties, officials believe that it would have cost at least a million dollars to deploy professional security analysts to find the vulnerabilities.[33]

---

33   https://www.pcmag.com/news/department-of-defenses-hack-the-pentagon-program-nets-138-issues

A collection of 8.4 billion passwords, the largest of all time, was leaked in 2021 in one of the world's popular hacker forums. The compilation was named "RockYou2021." With an estimated 4.7 billion people online in total, that cache of passwords is nearly twice global online population.[34]

Application Security Testing

Because every company is unique, there is no one-size-fits-all approach to application security. The right methodology is chosen based on risk exposure and the objective of the tests. Following are several commonly used methodologies.

- *Static application security testing (SAST)*

SAST is a security solution that helps find certain vulnerabilities in applications by analyzing source code and architecture while the application is being built. It is a white box technique that allows developers to identify security vulnerabilities early in the lifecycle.

- *Dynamic application security testing (DAST)*

DAST is a security solution that can help locate certain vulnerabilities in applications while they are running in production. It is a black box approach where the application is checked for potential vulnerabilities as an attacker would do — i.e., without knowing the internal code or architecture.

- *Interactive Application Security Testing (IAST)*

The IAST security solution combines DAST and SAST to find security vulnerabilities. IAST relies on an agent within the application to analyze

---

34   *https://cybernews.com/security/rockyou2021-alltime-largest-password-compilation-leaked/*

code dynamically while the app runs by an automated test, a human tester or any activity interacting with the application functionality.

- ***Runtime application self protection (RASP)***

RASP technology is plugged in to an application or its runtime environment. RASP incorporates security into a running application wherever it resides on a server. It intercepts all calls from the app to a system, making sure they are secure, and validates data requests directly inside the app.

Estonia is a small nation in the EU, bordered by Russia, Latvia and Finland. After its independence in 1991, the Estonian government decided to do something radical and focus their efforts on digital technologies. They created a digital id and proceeded to digitize all government operations to become the world's most advanced digital society.

The digital journey was not without roadblocks. In 2007, the country suffered a massive cyberattack[35] that brought down most of its infrastructure, provoked by the decision of the Estonian government to move a memorial to the Soviet Red Army to a position of less prominence. Cash machines, online banking services, media outlets and government bodies were sporadically taken down by botnets and huge amounts of internet traffic. Though it was not the first botnet strike, it was the first time the national security of an entire nation was threatened.

As Estonia found out, cyberthreats are a reality that represent some of the "modern" warfare that countries must face. Estonia now regards cybersecurity as an integral aspect of the digital lifestyle. Its determination to revolutionize cybersecurity has cemented its spot as one of the world leaders in the field.[36]

---

35   *https://en.wikipedia.org/wiki/2007_cyberattacks_on_Estonia*
36   *https://ncsi.ega.ee/ncsi-index/?order=rank*

CHAPTER 4

SPEED

"If an end user perceives bad performance from your website, her next click will likely be on your-competition.com." — Ian Molyneaux[37]

- - - - - - - - - - - - - - - -

As we all know, people tend to be impatient. In fact, according to a survey[38], 96% of Americans will knowingly consume extremely hot food or drink that burns their mouths and 63% do so frequently. Companies have made billions exploiting this tendency, and some have even found ways to make customers pay for their impatience. (One good example is priority boarding on airplanes.) When it comes to technology, our impatience seems to be greatly magnified, where any slight hiccup, pause, wait or latency is met by instant and intense displeasure. After all, technology comes with a promise of speed, and technology has helped create such high expectations that any failure to be fast enough could lose you many customers.

In the world of applications and other programs, sufficient speed means users never have to stare at a blank screen, never have to feel their attention wander and never deal with any mid-task breakdowns. Many applications struggle to deliver an acceptable level of performance along these lines.

---

37   https://www.goodreads.com/quotes/7078543-if-an-end-user-perceives-bad-performance-from-your-website
38   https://www.prnewswire.com/news-releases/ninety-six-percent-of-americans-are-so-impatient-they-knowingly-consume-hot-food-or-beverages-that-burn-their-mouths-finds-fifth-third-bank-survey-300026261.html

There are 2.39 million Android and 3.6 million iOS apps at the time of writing this book.[39] How many of them last more than 30 days in buyers' phones? Users discard the majority of apps as fast as they download them, and the number one reason is performance.

The only way to gauge whether your apps are sufficiently speedy, and whether they outpace your competitors' offerings is through continual performance evaluation and benchmarking.

Of course, some operations and transactions simply take a little longer computationally, and sometimes customers are willing to wait a few moments to get a personalized service, download a large document or fulfill a complex financial transaction. By studying and applying customer psychology, we could make the process feel shorter and less painful.

Why Do Elevators Have Mirrors?

In determining, an app's acceptable performance level, it is crucial to weigh the customers' *perceived* performance of the app even more than the actual performance. Perceived performance is a measure of how quick a user thinks your site or app is. Therefore, it is important to *measure from your customer's perspective, not just the server's.*

So why do elevators have mirrors? "Checking yourself out" was not the original intent. Earlier in the industrial era, high-rise buildings started to proliferate, for both residential and commercial purposes, and higher buildings made elevators essential. However, despite the fact that they did not have to climb stairs, people complained that the elevators were terribly slow and did not make their life better. Yet engineers found that the actual speed of the elevators was faster than an average human walking the stairs. So, what made them complain?

---

39   https://www.businessofapps.com/data/app-stores/

It was simply because of the appalling passenger experience of the elevator — closely confined, creaky, etc. A smart engineer approached the problem from a completely different angle by installing mirrors. Mirrors distracted passengers fretting about the speed and any with claustrophobia — essentially, they enhanced the user experience. Customers started to like the experience, and perceived elevators to be faster even though the speed hadn't changed. [40]

We can draw a parallel to this story in IT as well. Performance testing had always been about speed and load times. However, in the digital world it is all about experiences. The longer a site takes to load, the faster users leave. According to statistics, 47% of people expect your site to load in less than two seconds and 40% will abandon it entirely if it takes more than three seconds.[41] (This is equivalent to the elevator example.) One critical aspect of assuring right experience is to ensure that your app has the right performance. Thanks to smartphones and other gadgets, human attention spans are getting shorter. This means *you need to appeal to your customer in two seconds, delight them within eight and ultimately wow them in 20.*

> *Quick byte: Amazon found that it would lose $1.6 billion in sales each year if its page load slows by one second.[42]*

How to Improve on Wait Times

Ensuring you win your customers' continued attention lies in both improving absolute time performance and managing customers' perceptions. There are three key techniques to get this critical part of experience right:

---

40   https://platformliftco.co.uk/news-pr/why-do-lifts-have-mirrors
41   https://neilpatel.com/wp-content/uploads/2011/04/loading-time-sml.jpg
42   https://www.fastcompany.com/1825005/how-one-second-could-cost-amazon-16-billion-sales

Improve Perceived Performance

Perceived performance is a measure of how fast a user thinks your site is, which is often more important than its true speed. There are two kinds of time: *clock time* and *brain time*. The former is an objective measure; the latter is subjective — how a person *perceives* time. The best way to manage users' perception of time is to keep them in active mode.

Preloading Content

Preloading content and displaying content as soon as possible will give the impression that the page is fast. YouTube is a great example: It does not wait for the complete video to load, but instead starts streaming as soon as a minimum level of content is available. This reduces the necessity to buffer and often creates a perception of rapid streaming.

In many applications, users perform the same workflow repeatedly. This pattern can be used to predict users' next actions and thus to preload content. Right prioritization is required while preloading as too much content can increase the loading time, creating negative experiences. Though it may be tricky, well-executed preloading is well worth the effort for a better experience.

Instant Feedback

Providing users with *instant feedback* via animation or other visuals will keep them actively watching the progress. For anything that takes more than one second, a progress indicator is required to reduce uncertainty. A visual indicator that progresses toward completion puts the user at ease and increases their willingness to wait.

Variations of the visual display can have an impact. According to researchers from the Human Computer Interaction Institute at Carnegie Mellon University, varying the animations on progress bars creates the perception that the page is 11% faster.[43] Even simple tricks like starting the animation on the progress bar slowly in the beginning and having it accelerate as the end approaches will give a rapid sense of completion time for users.

Quell Anxiety at Every Step

Preparing the user is a key aspect of managing expectations. Telling the customer approximately how much time it will take for an order to be finalized after payment is completed will reduce any anxiety that customer might have. Such simple, clear text denoting exactly where users are in the process go a long way in improving customer experience.

Measure Perceived Performance

Since first interactions set the base for perceptions, it is vital to know when your app or site page is visually available, when it is actually interactive and when the customers interact with the page. Capturing such metrics with simple browser-based auditing tools does not even require heavy investment.

- **First paint (FP)**

FP is the time it takes for the browser to render the first pixel to a screen. It gives the impression to a user that the process is active but not necessarily able to be interacted with.

- **First contentful paint (FCP)**

FCP is how long it takes until the first piece of page content (text or image) is drawn in the browser window.

---

43   *https://www.chrisharrison.net/projects/progressbars2/*
ProgressBarsHarrison.pdf

Exhibit 8: Page content loading

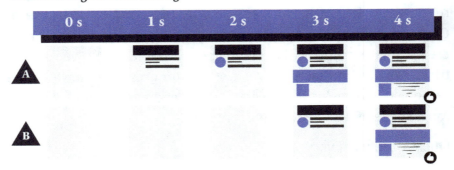

Exhibit 8 shows customer emotions while a website loads. The shorter the start render times, the better the experience for the user. The trick is to create a perception of speed by showing page elements as soon as possible.

- ***First meaningful paint (FMP)***

FMP is the amount of time it takes until useful content is rendered on the screen. What is deemed useful depends on the nature of your website and business objectives. Choice of content is also a critical factor. While *"a picture paints a thousand words,"* it is interesting images and visually appealing content that drag web performance down. Choosing the right image format combined with techniques such as lazy load and blurring the image before the full load happens can help diminish users' perception of idle time.

- ***Above-the-fold time (AFT)***

"Above the fold" is originally a newspaper term denoting the upper half of the paper which gets the most attention and thus is where the main stories are usually published. The same concept applies in the digital world. The area of "page" visible without scrolling — on any sized screen — gets the maximum views. AFT is the measure of how fast that content will load. The first step is to carefully define the target content, and then prioritize it to be loaded first, with the rest of the page soon following.

Actual Speed Is Still the Baseline

Though managing the *perceived* speed of your program or app is important in ensuring a positive experience, its baseline performance still depends on *actual* speed. According to estimates, a Facebook outage in 2021 cost the company about $164,000 a minute in revenue and lost market cap of $47.3 billion from the stock price tanking.[44] With such high-cost stakes and the potential reputational loss to your product and company from any downtime incidents, performance testing should be a critical step in your program/ application development process.

The RAIL Framework

RAIL stands for "response, animation, idle and load" — a model which Google developed[45] to measure each user interaction in its corresponding context. Users' expectations vary while performing different activities, and RAIL breaks down a user's experience into actions such as clicking a button, watching an animation, scrolling, waiting for a page to load, etc.

Every action that a user performs on the webpage is recorded and grouped into one of the RAIL categories.

- *Response*

Users expect instant responses of some kind when they click a button on a webpage. The experience is deemed well if a user does not see a lag or as long as their click is acknowledged in a reasonable amount of time. According to the RAIL model, *feedback in <100 milliseconds is within the acceptable range of desired experience.*[46]

---

44   *https://www.marketwatch.com/story/facebook-outage-by-the-numbers-largest-outage-ever-tracked-could-cost-millions-11633387093#:~:text=%E2%80%94%20Based%20on%20Facebook's%202020%20revenue,than%20six%20hours%20of%20downtime.*
45   *https://docs.google.com/presentation/d/13AJe2Ip4etqA8qylrva7bEgu1_hAvsq_VQiVOAxwdcI/htmlpresent*
46   *Ibid.*

- **Animation**

"Animations" comprise exit and entry animations, loading bars, scrolling, dragging and zooming. Users are sensitive to variations in animation speed, and so consistency is required to make visually appealing transitions. According to the model, *each animation should be completed in <16 milliseconds for a seamless experience.*[47]

- **Idle**

Idle work refers to things that happen in the background after the initial page load. Idle time is used to render the rest of the page's content or complete any backend processes. An effective way of minimizing idle time is by preloading content.

- **Load**

Load refers to getting the user to the first meaningful paint. Typically, *this should happen in <1sec.*

> ☺ Short Bytes
>
> *We have come a long way since the first website was launched, by British computer scientist Tim Berners-Lee in 1991. There are over 1.7 billion sites on the World Wide Web today. (However only 200 million are active.)*[48]

Performance Engineering

Performance engineering is a systematic, quantitative approach for the cost-effective development of software systems to meet performance requirements. It takes a shift-left approach to develop and tune software by testing against the required performance levels much earlier in the development process than conventional Waterfall approaches do. In performance engineering, the ultimate aim is to optimize customer experience, as earlier testing roots out glitches in the development phase rather than users finding them.

---

47   Ibid.
48   https://websitesetup.org/news/how-many-websites-are-there/

There are five key elements in performance engineering (see Exhibit 9) for us to examine.

Exhibit 9: Five elements of performance engineering

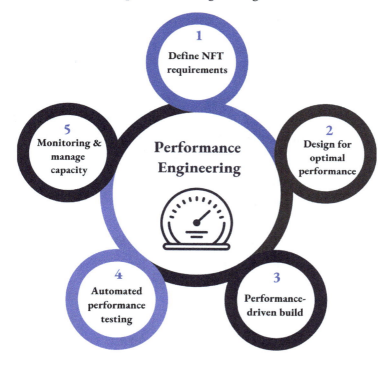

Define Nonfunctional Test Requirements

A *nonfunctional (NFT) requirement* is a requirement that specifies criteria to judge the operation of a system, rather than specific behaviors. It may address a property the product must possess, the standards by which it must be created or the environment in which it must exist. One of the qualities of a good requirement is that it is smart and testable. Precise statements explaining the behavior need to be specified before the build process.

"Only conducting performance testing at the conclusion of system or functional testing

Below are some common NFT requirements.

- **Scalability requirements**

Scalability is the ability of a system's capacity to grow or winnow down to meet the demand for its services. Scalability requirements can be classified based on components' architecture. For a user-intensive web application, the requirement could specify the maximum number of concurrent users it supports without performance impact. At the database level, it could be the number of queries it can process without performance degrading, and at the server level it could be the number of requests it supports without impacting response time. The advantage of identifying scalability requirements early in the SDLC is that it ensures that the architectural framework will be sound as the development proceeds.

- **Availability requirements**

All customers want an application to always be available. Though this is an obvious need for customer-facing applications, maintaining constant availability of all applications costs money and resources. It is therefore essential to be realistic in defining these requirements. Even an application that needs to be online 24/7 requires scheduled downtime for backups and maintenance. Availability requirements should also capture how long the system can be down when an outage happens — i.e., how long can the customer wait without experiencing too much frustration?

---

49   https://stepupautomation.wordpres s.com/2017/06/26/software-qa-quotes/

- *Reliability requirement*

Reliability measures time to failure or time between failures. This is easier to measure with mechanical products like car engines than it is with software. Mechanical components will eventually wear out and fail. Based on history and the projected lifetime of the components, one can determine the reliability of the engine. But measuring software reliability is trickier. Its reliability depends on the random occurrence of events and inputs under different states. A good reliability requirement should quantify the minimum value at which the customer would find the system unacceptable in the operational environment.

Design for Optimal Performance

An application's design is likely the single strongest determinant of its performance. In fact, many performance bottlenecks can be traced back to improper design and architecture. So enterprise architects face a daunting challenge — design all the dependent pieces of the application such as hardware, software, database, interfaces, modules, components, etc. to handle optimal performance.

Beyond that, however, involvement from the larger team (which should include both technical and business-aware members) is essential to bring in different perspectives and experience. Performance engineers can play a major role in aiding decision-making through rapid prototyping (which simulates how a particular system will perform in different configurations and interfaces) and by running performance scenarios to glean key insights. Collaboration between performance engineering and enterprise architecture is critical in effective design for optimal performance.

Performance-Driven Build

The next step in the lifecycle is to use the established performance objectives to build an application that meets the response time and throughput objectives. This stage is when a workload model is established, which defines load distributions across all identified scenarios.

- **Business workload**

A set of user actions or business scenarios performed to achieve defined business objectives and goals is called the *business workload*. This workload is represented as transactions per hour, including peak load periods and regular (daily, monthly) cycles.

- **Infrastructure workload**

The amount of resources or infrastructure used in the business scenarios to achieve the desired business goals is called the *infrastructure workload*. It determines the workload on the underlying infrastructure, CPU, memory, network utilization, etc.

Automated Performance Testing

In this step, performance tests are built to simulate the workload model. Realistically simulating the behavior and the number of end users is just one element for successfully testing performance. The other essential part is to constantly run performance scripts to detect and mitigate performance issues before they have a chance to derail the application. Integrating performance testing in the continuous integration pipeline has become a necessity.

The ultimate objective of performance testing is to mitigate risks. But there are many types of performance testing around (see Figure XX to see Exhibit 10). Choosing the right test for your application depends on which particular ability of the software you want to measure.

Exhibit 10: Types of performance tests

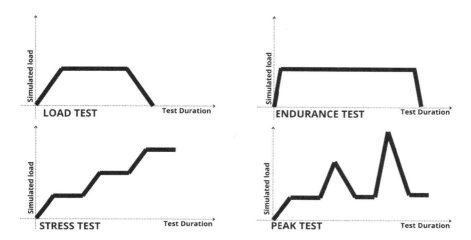

- **Load test**

Load testing measures system performance as the workload increases under normal conditions — "normal conditions" meaning the calculated load of customers or transactions your application is expected to handle until it hits a breaking point.

- **Stress test**

Stress testing measures system performance outside of the parameters of normal working conditions. The objective of such testing is to find out the upper threshold, or breaking point, of the application by simulating more transactions than expected. Stress testing also measures how your application copes in that situation.

- **Volume test**

In this database-focused test, the database is flooded with huge volumes of data, and performance levels such as server throughput and response times are monitored.

- **Scalability test**

Scalability testing measures an application's ability to scale up or down. Scalability can be measured at the hardware, software or database levels. It is usually performed as a series of load tests, and consequences are measured against predetermined parameters.

- *Endurance test*

Endurance testing measures how your application performs with a normal workload over an extended period of time. The objective is to find out the side effects of prolonged exposure to loads from memory leaks, system crashes, etc.

Monitor & Manage Capacity

Monitoring is the systematic and routine collection of information about the applications' hardware and software operations to ensure everything functions as expected. In modern software development, it is a requirement, not a choice. Basic monitoring involves collecting performance statistics, response times, errors, CPU usage, availability, etc. Capturing the right metrics is a critical step in integrating performance engineering within your organization. Always bear in mind that the metrics that matter most are those that measure things that make your customers happy — speed, reliability, etc.

There are two common approaches to monitoring: passive and active. Though they differ, and each has advantages and disadvantages, they often complement each other. Using both methods paints a full picture for understanding the end-user experience.

- *Active or synthetic monitoring*

Active monitoring simulates a user's behavior and navigation paths in an app or program. It provides information on the app's uptime, availability and performance. Active monitoring is increasingly popular because of its "real-time" nature and independence from actual user traffic: While real user traffic only shows how your app performs in existing conditions, active monitoring can simulate future states.

Active monitoring also can be equipped with machine learning algorithms to analyze current log data in order to predict and simulate possible future conditions.

While this method is precise, targeted and well-suited for real-time troubleshooting and optimization, its downside is that since it uses simulated traffic, it can never 100% represent actual traffic — and thus the real customer experience.

- *Passive monitoring*

Passive monitoring tracks actual traffic over a period of time. Though the objective is the same as active monitoring, there is an obvious difference between a script, which runs in machine speed, and how a human interacts with the application. The observational nature of passive monitoring makes it ideal for determining the current baseline statistics, which are then extrapolated to simulate expected conditions. Also, the "sniffing" approach of passive monitoring can provide rich user details like location, browser, device, etc. — which provide valuable inputs for troubleshooting.

Passive monitoring is mandatory for mission-critical applications where failure can have far-reaching implications.

So, to summarize, active monitoring is the more proactive approach which prevents problems from happening and passive monitoring provides the baseline for it. Clearly, a hybrid approach is ideal to ensure that customers get a seamless experience.

- *Capacity management*

Capacity management means right-sizing IT resources to meet current and future needs in a cost-effective manner. Effective capacity management is proactive not reactive: It uses simulation and automation to make real-time adjustments to resources as needed to accommodate changing workloads. In-depth analysis of the monitoring data is used to spot changes in demand and tune the infrastructure configurations accordingly. For example, noncritical workloads can be moved to off-peak hours or extra infrastructure can be dynamically allocated during peak hours.

> 🙂 Short Bytes
>
> *With a theoretical peak performance of 537 petaFLOPs, Fugaku is the world's fastest supercomputer. Fugaku has achieved a speed of more than 440 quadrillion transactions per second.*[50]

---

50   *https://www.fujitsu.com/global/about/innovation/fugaku/*

Experiences that Delight

WHAT DELIGHTS CUSTOMERS?

Part I outlined the qualities that appeal to customers, the fundamental attributes that induce them to buy your app, product or service. But making the sale is just half the battle. The other half is to produce delight once they start using the product, which means *exceeding expectations every time*. Such delight is essential in building long-term relationships with customers, and the QA function is, as always, a key ingredient for establishing and maintaining these durable connections. (Meanwhile, the "wow factor," which we shall address in Part III of the book, seals the deal through outstanding, cutting-edge qualities.).

So, what delights a customer?

Among the essential elements that produce delight in today's digital world — that go the extra distance to exceed customer expectations — are the trifecta of quality, speed and cost. A common fallacy[51] in project management is that we can only have two of the three at any time. But our digital world demands all three be in place. The good news is that the three elements are interconnected: When an organization produces and performs at the right quality, it can deliver faster (as rework effort is minimal) and thereby reduce costs.

At this stage in our digital evolution, another key delightful quality, and competitive differentiator, is omnichannel connectivity — which represents a major shift from a single channel world. Although customers tend to use each channel — the web, mobile, chat, etc. — for different purposes, what delights them is the consistent experience they get across the channels.

---

51   *https://www.digitalbrew.com/quality-speed-price-unattainable-triangle/*

The transformation journey is a continual activity, and *the levers of a delightful customer experience are continuous measurement, innovation and an ongoing effort to improve quality.*

CHAPTER 5

FREQUENCY

*"An organization's journey to excellence begins once it
ceases to sacrifice quality for speed."[52]*
—*Neil Beyersdorf, Quality, Risk & Change Management
Consultant*

- - - - - - - - - - - - - - - - - -

In our hyper-accelerated world, merely having a great idea or innovative product hardly guarantees success — unless an organization can also bring the product to market before its competition gets there with something similar, or even better. Further, consumers are notoriously fickle: Anything more than a year old is considered outdated and fails to excite customers anymore. This compels the business to continually innovate with new and better features to compete effectively and enhance its perceived value.

However, a company can be severely damaged by rolling out features that don't interest customers — or, even worse, any that fail to work, even occasionally. Speedy rollouts are great, but if quality is lacking or flawed, such swiftness is just counterproductive.

For those old enough to remember, "*It's a Kodak moment*" strikes a nostalgic chord. But along with the phrase comes the memory of how Kodak, once a household name, went bankrupt by failing to adapt to digitalization. What's interesting is that Kodak actually invented the first digital camera, in 1975 (see photo); but it was Sony that

---

52   *https://www.slideshare.net/optimaltransformation/an-organizations-journey-to-excellence-begins-once-it-ceases-to-sacrifice-quality-for-speed-neil-beyersdorf*

introduced a digital camera suitable for the masses. As mentioned above, hitting the market first with new inventions and products is not sufficient to be successful. The quality of the product, and how well it is attuned to customer experience, are paramount.

A better formula for success, we find, are companies that continuously entice the customers with frequent new feature releases. These organizations are often more successful than the first entrants in a market. In the quest for competitive speed and innovation, the IT world has adopted the mantra, *"Release often, release early."*

Exhibit 11: The world's first digital camera

For companies to effectively compete, continuous improvements are required, with each iteration of the application an improvement on quality and CX.

However, even though customers are more demanding nowadays and expect cool new features as often as possible, newly released features with shortfalls in quality will make them very unhappy. According to Toptal, a whopping 88% of online customers won't return if they have a bad experience.[53] In sum, keeping the balance between speed and quality is all about balancing innovation and CX. So, the conundrum

---

53   https://www.toptal.com/designers/ux/ux-statistics-insights-infographic

for business is, *How do you develop and market your products right away, and in the right way?*

How to Accelerate Quality

Reducing time-to-market cannot be achieved by merely changing one function or digitizing a single department. Rather, it takes the concerted, collective efforts of multiple departments and teams to bring forth systematic change. And QA always must be a central concern. Our specific focus is on quality aspects that enable companies to bring features to market faster and thus enhance CX. Quality at speed is a result of two factors:

◆ *Continuous automated quality assurance*
◆ *Shattering dependencies and automation bottlenecks*

Continuous Automated Assurance

Continuous assurance is the process of automatically checking every quality aspect of product development, and obtaining immediate feedback on product usability. This is possible only with continuous automation. Continuous automated QA ensures that the product is always built in the right way throughout the development lifecycle by executing automated tests, checks and controls.

The goal of continuous assurance is to create repeatable, reliable and automated end-to-end processes, beginning from writing clear user stories to delivering an optimal product to customers.

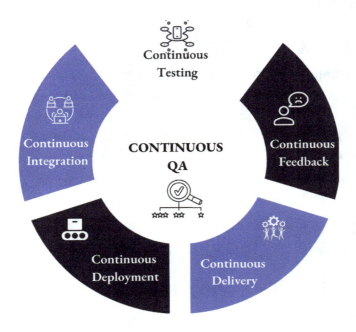

Streamlined customer experience arises elegantly from a smart, automated experience assurance strategy. In fact, we think traditional test automation should shift gears and focus on more aspects of product development right from ideation to customer support. The following areas and activities are necessary to set up continuous assurance in your organization.

The Quality Pipeline

A quality pipeline is simply the sequence of activities or tasks performed to ensure quality at every stage of development, starting from product ideation all the way to delivery to customers and afterwards. Each step in the pipeline (see Figure XX) is an automated process that handles a different aspect of quality.

Exhibit 13: The quality pipeline

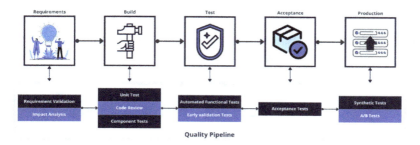

Quality Pipeline

The overall quality pipeline is often subdivided and tackled using different sub-pipelines. The *feature pipeline*, for example, breaks down ideas into concrete requirements that are easy to interpret and develop. The *build pipeline* starts as soon as a developer submits a piece of code. The chunk of code is integrated into the central code base, which sequentially activates several unit test runs. When an integration test proves successful, a binary file is created which is passed on to subsequent stages. This file is then subjected to a vigorous round of system, regression, performance and security testing in the *release pipeline,* which deploys the binary in different stages in different environments.

Undoubtedly, ever-increasing automation helps with faster product go-to-market delivery. But automating QA is grueling, and demands specialized skillsets and resources. In particular, mastering test automation has been a daunting task in the past decade.

Test Automation

Test automation is an integral part of continuous assurance. Although test automation has been in place for several years, it remained rudimentary in many organizations. There are several reasons why organizations struggle to scale up test automation.

Why Test Automation Fails

The number-one reason for test automation failure is a lack of understanding of its actual nature. It is far more than just automating tests that would otherwise run manually. Rather, it involves automating the entire process, with infrastructure and technology simplification.

According to the 2020 State of Test Automation report by Perfecto,[54] test coverage is a top challenge for the teams. The average test automation coverage is less than 50% across industries. It is high time to rethink and reevaluate automation strategy.

There are five common reasons for the failure of automation.

- **Lack of sufficient time**

Historically, time allocated for testing has been very limited. Even with today's Agile methodology and teams, active testing of user stories generally happens only in the last few days of the Sprint. There are several reasons for this: Building larger requirements takes more time before they are available for testing. Especially when Agile teams are at work, requirements need to be broken down into smaller chunks to create a minimum viable product ready for early testing. But testing, by its nature, is an afterthought activity — one that is too often rushed. After all, we need to have the product ready before we start testing.

- **Lack of technical skills**

Creating stable, repeatable tests is an art that requires highly trained technical artisans. In fact, however, most teams don't have the required skill set. A direct consequence of lack of technical skills are flaky tests — tests that pass and fail periodically without any code changes. Flakiness in the tests can be attributed to poor object locaters used in the code and the inability of testers to programmatically handle varying page load times. Scriptless tools used for test automation play a significant role in bridging the skill gap.

---

54   *https://www.perfecto.io/sites/perfecto/files/pdfs/report-perfecto-2020-state-of-test-automation.pdf*

- *Frequent changes*

With the prevalence of the Agile methodology, development teams are increasingly handling new features and changes than ever before. These frequent changes to the code base require several rounds of refactoring and continuous maintenance. Many development teams ignore the accumulated technical debt, and product owners fail to prioritize such debt stories.

The situation is the same with automation scripts. By taking in more changes, the automation code requires continuous refactoring as well. Many test teams fail to manage change easily, as sometimes it takes more time to refactor test automation code than to write the application code itself.

Also, management tends to misunderstand and thus underestimate the actual effort required in building robust tests. This is because traditionally, only a fraction or a percentage of the development effort was allotted for testing.

- *Poor design*

The stability of test automation depends on the testability of an application. Writing awesome test automation scripts is not enough; the application and its architecture need to be supported as well. One of the simplest examples is the use of unique meaningful identifiers, as a customer would see the object while using the webpage. It is not only intuitive for the testers but also brings in a *human-centric approach* where design, build and tests are performed from the customer's perspective.

Get Your Automation Back on Track

Fortunately, there are practical steps available today to reassess your automation strategy and get it back on track.

- *Use static code analyzers*

Code is *holy* in test automation. It is important to maintain high standards and readability to get a stable automation suite running.

Use simple static code analyzers that can report most common errors, deviations from coding standards, redundant code, etc.

- *Use standard libraries*

With test automation, *less coding is more*. Quality engineers often tend to err by writing custom code to solve any deviant task not supported by the tool or framework used. Custom-built functions are susceptible to complexity and brittleness when compared to off-the-shelf modules. Instead of reinventing the wheel, it is better to check the market for availability of similar functions or modules.

- *Separate data from code*

Stable automation scripts require access to the right data. In a data-driven test (DDT) approach, data is externalized and stored in databases or files. This externalized data feeds the automation. The advantage of externalizing data is that the same tests can be run with different sets of data. For example, both positive and negative conditions can be tested with different data.

- *Follow the Boy Scout rule*

We all know the rule: "Always leave the campground cleaner than you found it." This also applies to any code, be it for test automation or application development. Constant refactoring is required to make the code better than it was. The rule applies both to code that you personally wrote as well as the code that your peers wrote — i.e., do not fall prey to the common tendency to improve only your own code.

- *Choose the right scripting language*

As a generic rule, test automation scripting employs the same programming language used to develop the application. There are two common reasons for this:

- *Introducing a new programming language requires extra support and sometimes infrastructure.*
- *Application developers can help the test automation engineers with their expertise on the programming language.*

However, this generic "rule" need not be followed. Test automation development is not the same as application development in terms of complexity or scale. So sometimes, it is better to choose a scripting language that is simple, easy to learn and easy to program with.

- ***Cross browser testing***

Browsers are all somewhat different; this is why some highly praised "user-friendly" actions work on certain browsers and misbehave or fail completely on others. Plus, browsers are subject to continuous updates, and it is important to shield the product against these changes. Therefore, it is essential to test all the significant customer journeys in the most used/supported browsers.

But it might be too time-consuming to support and maintain every kind of browser each time there is a product or feature upgrade. The company should have a clear specification on what browsers to support and for how long.

> 😊 Short Bytes
>
> *Upon finding a moth inside the Harvard Mark II computer on Sept. 9th, 1947, Grace Murray Hopper logged the first ever "bug" in history. Though there are controversies whether this was the first time the word was ever used for computer problems, it certainly made the term popular.[55]*

Continuous Feedback

Waiting until the end of a Sprint is too long to solicit feedback. The speed of the feedback loops determines how fast you can create meaningful features for customers. Feedback loops tell the teams

---

55   https://www.nationalgeographic.org/thisday/sep9/worlds-first-computer-bug/

whether their development efforts are fruitful, and how satisfied customers are. In other words, there are two critical feedback loops for continuous feature development — one at the technical level and the other from end users themselves.

Technical Feedback

- ***Availability monitoring***

Availability measures the extent to which an application or service is accessible for fulfilling users' or business requirements. Availability monitoring prevents adverse situations by checking the uptime of infrastructure components such as servers, applications, interfaces, etc., and notifying users when incidents occur. Though availability monitoring is widely executed in production environments, it is also essential for development environments.

Customer Feedback

Most companies know how to collect feedback from customers. The real challenge is creating a continuous feedback loop where the responses translate into concrete actions and are incorporated in product development.

Customer feedback deserves consideration alongside strategic product priorities. Similarly, the value of the feedback is not just in finding out what features the customer needs but also in synthesizing the learnings from that feedback proactively for future product development.

Shatter the Dependencies & Accelerate

In addition to automation issues, a number of other bottlenecks can hinder the objective of delivering features faster to customers. Having the right data, representative environment, defined methodology and scalable automation complemented by a continuous monitoring system are key ingredients in a continuous quality pipeline.

Technical Skills: Go Scriptless

Writing stable automation tests requires good technical skills. *Scriptless* test automation is a technique that eliminates or reduces the need for writing code to automate test cases. Going scriptless not only helps to overcome technical challenges but also enables bringing together people with different skillsets, such as manual testers with functional expertise, business, operations, etc. Even people with little or no technical skills can contribute to test automation when a scriptless approach is used.

- *Maintainability*

Maintainability defines how code can be modified, adapted or transferred from one development team to another, while readily meeting new business requirements. Scriptless test automation provides reusable components and well-structured methods for implementing automated testing. This facilitates making changes to the test suite when the software being tested changes, as the maintenance phase is usually the longest.

- *Reliability*

Reliability defines how long a system can run without failure. Many of the arguments against scriptless testing come from the early days of test automation when recorded tests were often flaky, unrepeatable and not reusable. Significant development has happened since then and today's scriptless tools are robust and use a combination of techniques to make automation scripts more reliable.

- *Collaborative*

The scriptless nature of test automation facilitates collaboration with business and subject matter experts in addition to technical staff.

- *Scriptless tools*

There are a handful of commercial and free scriptless tools in the market. The criteria for choosing a tool are the type of technology involved, the skillsets of the people using it and the scale of operations.

Continuous Environment

A continuous test environment is a necessity to achieve continuous automation. Many companies don't realize how imperative a stable environment is for automation and to increase efficiency. With cloud and container technologies becoming more reliable, the developer world can build stable scalable environments now.

> 😊 Short Bytes
>
> *The cloud computing concept dates back to the 1960s. The phrase originates from that era, when the cloud symbol was used in flowcharts and diagrams to symbolize the internet.*

Leverage the Cloud

According to Microsoft, cloud computing is the delivery of computing services — servers, storage, databases, networking, software, analytics, intelligence, etc. — over the internet ("the cloud") to offer faster innovation, flexible resources and economies of scale.[56]

A well-configured test environment that has the right data and that closely mimics the production environment would be a blessing for any test engineer. Such an ideal environment was elusive for testers for many years and for various reasons, like interdependencies, complexity, storage, costs, etc. Cloud services are usually offered in a pay-per-use model for resources, which lowers costs for businesses. There are a number of common cloud service models.

---

56   *https://azure.microsoft.com/en-us/overview/what-is-cloud-computing/*

- **_Infrastructure-as-a-Service (Host)_**

IaaS provides highly automated and scalable compute resources with scalable storage and network capability. Spinning out virtual machines to set up test environments on demand is a great way to solve the age-old problem of infrastructure unavailability.

- **_Platform-as-a-Service (Build)_**

PaaS provides a platform for software creation. PaaS makes the development, testing and deployment of applications quick, simple and cost-effective.

- **_Software-as-a-Service (Consume)_**

SaaS is a software distribution model where the service provider hosts the software in its data center and the customer can access it over the internet. It represents the largest component of the cloud market. The provider manages access to the application, including security, availability and performance. Usage of tools on demand for application development and testing is another element of SaaS.

> 😊 **Short Bytes**
>
> _How big is the cloud? By 2025, 100 zettabytes[57] of data will be stored in the cloud. Remember the days when gigabytes were considered to be a huge amount of storage space? To visualize it, a zettabyte is 1,000 exabytes, and a single exabyte can hold roughly 36,000 years' worth of HD quality video or stream the entire Netflix catalog over 3,000 times._

Advantages of the Cloud

Cloud-based test tools increase the scope of browsers, and provide on-demand hardware and environments to speed up the test process. There are several advantages.

---

57   _https://cybersecurityventures.com/the-world-will-store-200-zettabytes-of-data-by-2025/_

- *Availability*

Availability of environments was the biggest complaint area on the IT development floor for many years, yet little was done to resolve it. Improved availability and decreased downtime and outages are some of the biggest benefits of moving to cloud-based infrastructure and applications. The inherent elastic and managed nature of the cloud can immediately solve many of the headaches in guaranteeing availability.

- *Scalability*

Scalability is the cloud's biggest single advantage. It means testers can scale (up or down) computing resources based on need. This is especially useful when multiple resources are consumed during peak execution hours.

- *Cost reduction*

The hardware and license costs can quickly ramp up, especially for larger teams and big organizations. Since most of the cloud services work on the pay-for-use model, they can be easily scaled up and down to meet requirements. This eliminates the need for heavy resources and hardware, which would remain underutilized most of the time.

- *Speed*

Cloud-based tools enable companies to bring their applications to production faster by offering gains in productivity and time savings.

- *Cross-browser/device/OS*

Working in the cloud, testers have a wide choice of devices, browsers and operating systems. Testing on multiple devices ensures that applications work on a variety of machines. It also eliminates the need to procure multiple devices per team, which helps shave costs.

Containerization

Containerization is a method of isolating and encapsulating an application in its own operating environment — which is lighter, faster and quicker to start than a virtual machine. Containers give developers the ability to create predictable environments that are isolated from other applications.

With this approach, developers don't have to pull the application code and deploy it in the test environment each time; rather, testing can be done against the container image. Containers make it easy to simulate a production-like environment in the developer's machine.

Parallelization can speed up testing several-fold. In the past, the limited number of available machines and hardware meant tests would sometimes be run sequentially — which is a highly ineffective use of resources and time. Containers enable large-scale automation and parallelization, the two key elements to accelerate testing.

> 😊 Short Bytes
>
> *Norman Joseph Woodland helped invent the barcode, receiving a patent for it in 1952. However, it was not until 22 years later that the barcode application for product labelling was developed. The first product scanned was a package of chewing gum, in 1974.*[58]

---

58   https://www.barcodesinc.com/news/what-is-the-first-product-to-ever-have-a-barcode/

CHAPTER 6

CONNECTIVITY

"If you think that the internet has changed your life, think again. The Internet of Things is about to change it all over again!"[59] — Brendan O'Brien, Co-founder and Chief Innovation Officer, Aria Systems

----

Communication is intrinsic to life on earth, and we continue to discover new communicational networks in nature.[60] Ever since humans developed some kind of formal communication system — roughly three million years after our human ancestors evolved — communication has been the driving force in cultural and technological growth.[61]

In the digital age, the boundaries between human and machine are becoming blurred. With the advancement in voice recognition technologies, for example, humans now speak directly to machines through voice commands and other gestures. Meanwhile, machines have rapidly become more intelligent and have started to communicate with each other in their digital language.

The still-accelerating evolution in communications has resulted in a phenomenon called *hyper-connectivity*. Hyper-connectivity refers not only to the technical impacts of communications and devices but also the resultant personal and organizational changes. Even in our

59   https://www.ariasystems.com/blog/internet-things-quotes-consider/
60   https://www.smithsonianmag.com/science-nature/the-whispering-trees-180968084/
61   https://www.creativedisplaysnow.com/articles/history-of-communication-from-cave-drawings-to-the-web/

own lifetimes, we have seen telephones going wireless and merging with computers that fit in our pockets, the cloud becoming virtually ubiquitous, communication lines getting far shorter, and much else. Resultant changes include the phenomenon of being always on, always connected and always distracted. We've all seen the behavioral shifts.

Indeed, our newly hyper-connected reality makes it is undeniable that the world is undergoing a *Fourth Industrial Revolution*[62]. The First Industrial Revolution was heralded by the advent of steam power and the transition from hand tools to machine tools. The Second Industrial Revolution was driven by mass production in factories on assembly lines. The Third Industrial Revolution, or Industry 3.0, was about incorporating robotics and computers to drive basic automation and straight-through processes.

Our current revolution, *Industry 4.0,* refers to the shift to interconnectivity, advanced automation, machine learning and other forms of AI, etc. Industry 4.0 has meant the opportunity to network machines and aggregate data in the form of analytical dashboards that can inform actions. Originating in Germany, and fueled by the booming Internet of Things, Industry 4.0 represents a massive change in how humans and machines interact.

62   *https://www.weforum.org/agenda/2016/01/the-fourth-industrial-revolution-what-it-means-and-how-to-respond/*

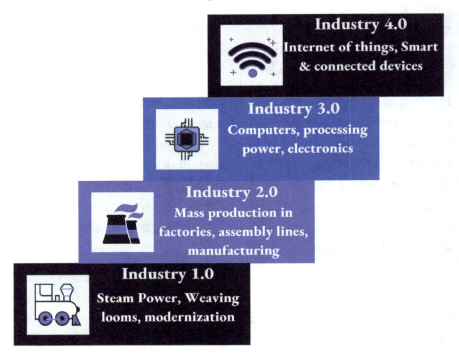

Internet of Things (IoT)

The *IoT* is the use of intelligently connected devices and systems to leverage data gathered by embedded sensors and actuators in machines and other physical objects. IT and business leaders at many companies have realized that IoT is not merely a technological experiment to connect devices, but rather a driver of digital transformation for their own companies and even their entire industry.

IoT's potential is immense; so far, we have only scratched the surface. Its impact will only grow as it brings together the worlds of machines and humans. What began with smart phones has now spread to smart homes, smart toys, smart watches, smart assistants, etc.

IoT can even overhaul companies outside the typical IT digital spectrum. For example, the waste management company Bigbelly has transformed waste collection and management industry by connecting their smart trashcans with simple sensors.[63] These connected trashcans (see Exhibit 15) have saved many thousands of dollars in fuel, labor costs, etc. by letting collectors know when the cans are exactly full and require service. Sweden has installed talking Bigbelly smart waste stations in the city of Västerås to encourage users and improve experiences.

Exhibit 15: The Bigbelly bins

Another example, from the retail industry, is Tommy Hilfiger's use of blue tooth chips and sensors to track movements and reward users for wearing them.[64] Customers can compete in challenges and thus amass points that can be exchanged for discounts and charities in the store. Not only does IoT provide customers with unique experiences, but it also involves customers in the brand experience.

---

63   https://bigbelly.com/
64   https://wwd.com/fashion-news/fashion-scoops/tommy-hilfiger-launches-tommy-jeans-xplore-1202764296/

Exhibit 16: The IoT ecosystem evolution

| Device | Smart Device | Connected Device | IoT Ecosystem |

Types of IoT

- ***Consumer IoT***

IoT applications in this sector involve personal and home automation tools designed for individuals or groups. Popular consumer IoT applications include smart homes, wearables and personal assistants. According to the research from GSMA, enterprise IoT will take over consumer IoT connections in 2024 and will triple between 2018 and 2025, to $13.3 billion. Nevertheless, consumer IoT will remain a crucial area for CX, as the human/machine interface is the cutting edge.[65]

- ***Industrial IoT (IIoT)***

IIoT differs from consumer IoT in that it is used in commercial and industrial applications — such as oil pipelines, manufacturing machines and aircraft engines. Accordingly, industrial IoT sensors are designed to handle extreme weather conditions and corrosive environments. Also, the number of data points in an industrial IoT can be in the millions or billions, which requires huge data handling capacity.

Quality Challenges

Hyper-connectivity, fueled by the rise of smart devices and IoT, vastly increases interactions not only among humans but also between humans and machines. Such a quantum leap in the proliferation of

---

65   *https://www.gsma.com/iot/resources/iot-connections-forecast-the-rise-of-enterprise/*

connected devices and communication channels poses a unique challenges for ensuring quality and enhancing experience.

For starters, today's testing and development methodologies, languages and tools are poorly suited to face the growing technical hurdles arising from millions or billions of interconnected devices. Comprehensive quality and compliance strategies are essential to address the challenges posed by each of the following areas.

- **Platforms**

IoT platforms comprise the support software that connects everything in an IoT ecosystem. With an abundance of software, firmware and hardware platform variants, testing for all possible combinations is impractical and far from foolproof.

- **Protocols**

Machine-to-machine and machine-to-server communication is enabled by standard communication protocols, such as MQTT, XMPP, CoAP, AMQP, etc. A fundamental reason the IoT ecosystem is so incredibly complex is the lack of protocol standardization. Further, connected IoT devices need to interface with different wireless standards like Wi-Fi, Bluetooth, ZigBee, 4G, etc. Therefore, it is important to test the different standards to ensure their reliability and security for communication between controllers and disparate devices.

- **Simulation difficulties**

IoT is a dense combination of protocols, devices, operating systems, firmware and hardware, networking layers. Yet *IoT simulation* is necessary for performance planning, what-if scenarios, security evaluations, etc. The very scale of the IoT — with its vast number of current nodes plus exponential increases in complexity when devices are added — makes it extremely difficult for existing simulation tools to recreate.

- **Lack of standards & certifications**

As we have emphasized, there is a nearly overwhelming array of connectivity options to sort through for electronics engineers and application developers working on IoT products and systems. Unfortunately, however, there is so far a chronic lack of standardization in the IoT industry. Each manufacturer builds devices as per its own requirements, which can (and will) result in conflicting standards and interconnectivity issues.

> 😊 Short Bytes
>
> *The number of IoT devices is predicted to grow dramatically to 75 billion devices in 2025 — and to explode to 125 billion devices by 2030. That means on average there will be 15 things connected to the internet for every human on earth.[66] Of course, a mega-system like that entails large risk exposure: A lot of things can go wrong.*

How to Ensure IoT Quality

Your application is a de facto "experience platform" that connects the customer and your organization, and quality plays a central role in ensuring the platform provides a satisfying experience. Whereas traditional app development had been on web and mobile platforms, working with connected devices means handling a plethora of different platforms — and your quality management system must be up to the job.

CX makes all the difference in terms of users embracing or rejecting IoT devices. The whole point of bringing IoT devices into one's home is greater ease of use and more convenience than old-world unconnected devices afforded. And it should offer a positive benefit to your life to be able, for example, to manage your home's lighting or heating remotely or to have your smart assistant read you the

---

66   *https://www.nanowerk.com/smart/internet-of-things-explained.php*

day's calendar appointments out loud. However, if poor functionality means your IoT devices make one's life harder rather than easier, that defeats the purpose.

Assuring quality CX with IoT devices calls for the following three activities:

◆ *Creating digital twins*
◆ *Interface & interoperability testing*
◆ *Compliance & device certification*

Creating Digital Twins

A *digital twin* is a virtual representation of a physical object or system across its lifecycle (design, build, operate) using real-time operational data and other sources to enable understanding, learning, reasoning and dynamically re-calibrating for improved decision making. The physical object can be anything from a building to a ball bearing, and the system (or systems) can be electrical, mechanical, software, etc. According to an industry report,[67] up to 91% of all IoT platforms will contain some form of digital capability by 2026 and will become a standard feature of IoT applications by 2028.

So the question of the moment is: *How does one create a digital twin?* The creation process starts with determining what exactly needs to simulated and what data is required to enable that simulation. Building digital twins can be a daunting prospect, but at a high level can be broken down into three stages.

▪ *Design*

The design process starts with engineers choosing the right technology to be "twinned" and determining what data needs to be collected from the physical device — and how. The amount of data that can be collected through sensors from a physical system is enormous.

---

67   https://www.researchandmarkets.com/reports/5308850/digital-twins-market-by-technology-twinning

To build a twin that has the highest potential to reap rewards, answer these questions: *What is the most crucial insight that you would gain? What data and process would provide most value to the company and result in maximum efficiency?*

Another critical question in designing a digital twin solution is the level of detail required. The best approach would be to start with a basic, simple design and scale up as the model evolves.

- **Development**

During the development stage, the aggregated data from different systems is analyzed and visualized. Driven by analytics, a mathematical model that simulates the physical asset's behavior and performance is developed. The model generates insights by processing the data collected, which helps guide decision making.

- **Operation**

Once an initial version of the digital twin has been created, it can be run in a production environment, such as a shop floor. Creating a digital twin is not a one-off process, but rather requires continuous evaluation of goals and potential improvements based on the insights gathered. Once the digital twin is in operation, actionable data is fed back to the physical asset and actions are taken through actuators. When the intended objective of the digital twin is achieved, the process can be scaled up to larger systems, machines, buildings or even the enterprise as a whole.

Exhibit 17: Digital twin

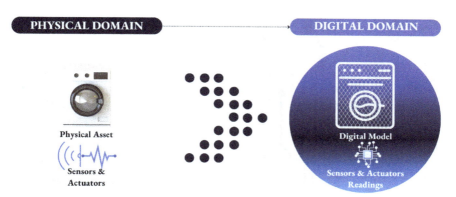

Interface & Interoperability Testing

Interoperability is a system's ability to work with or use parts of another system seamlessly. Such interoperability and connectivity are crucial for IoT, and differentiate this technology from ordinary computer-driven machinery. And many of the interfaces and communications are impossible without APIs.

Application Program Interfaces (APIs)

Essentially, an API provides a set of clearly defined definitions, methods, protocols and functions for program components to connect to each other. Although APIs have been around since the 1960s, they have gained greatly increasing importance with the growing digitization of our world. In the connected-device ecosystem we all now dwell in, every device needs an API. Without APIs, the digital experience of today would not be possible.

In fact, APIs in many ways drive and control companies' profitability, resulting in a new paradigm called the *API economy*. According to Gartner, "The API economy is an enabler for turning a business or organization into a platform." And platforms enable companies to connect to the ecosystem by sharing their assets with the community.

How APIs Help Improve Experience

Across industries, APIs render customers' digital journeys seamless, and so they form a critical component in CX. As the communication language between applications, APIs not only enable organizations to make their features available to the world but also provide valuable insights on who is using the APIs and in what ways and volumes.

APIs' rise has even prompted traditional financial companies to offer their services as APIs. With the introduction of the Second Payment Services Directive (PSD2) in 2018, banks are obligated to make transaction data available for third parties (assuming the customer provides consent). This has been a game changer, forcing banks to move toward open banking where all bank services are available as APIs for third parties to consume. PSD2 puts the customer, not the transaction, at the center of the payment process. With smart devices like Google Home, Alexa and others rapidly maturing, it is only a short step till these APIs can be triggered via voice to make payments from the convenience of your home for instance.

One perfect example of a company orchestrating APIs to create a new profitable business model is Uber. For Uber to work requires many components: At minimum, it needs to know the customer's exact location, the location of the driver, the distance between them and the best routes, and must provide a means of customer and driver to communicate with each other, and for payments to be made. Building all those functional components would have been a huge undertaking of time, effort and money. Uber chose to avoid the extreme complexities and opted to consume APIs from different providers instead. Mapkit and Google Maps APIs provide route calculations, the Braintreee API handles payments, Twilio provides communication and MailChimp's Mandrill API handles receipts. As this example clearly shows, APIs now function as veritable Lego blocks to construct the modern digital economy.

Microservices & Contracts

Increasingly popular in the land of APIs, microservices are an architectural style that structures an application as a collection of services which are autonomously deployable and modular, which represent a unique process, and which connect via a well-defined and lightweight mechanism. Tech giants such as Netflix, Spotify and Amazon adopted microservices to enable them to scale quickly and rapidly adapt to market needs. These companies maintain a strong CX perspective while building their microservices.

If one of the smaller microservices fails, the impact is low. The key is finding all such failures as early as possible in order to build a resilient ecosystem.

Though microservices are quite efficient, they present a unique challenge for QA testers. The biggest complexity is not within the microservices themselves, but on how these services interact with each other to provide a seamless experience.

Microservices Quality Challenges

It is always tempting to set up an environment for end-to-end tests with connections to all applications and interfaces, and then perform tests to verify the functionality of the whole system. This is often a good way to verify the features work across the chain before deploying to production.

However, these environments are expensive to maintain, and dependencies are hard to manage due to their great complexity. This results in failing and unpredictable tests. Also writing end-to-end tests is difficult and very time-consuming. More complex tests demand more time and effort, and they often become brittle if not maintained continuously.

The manufacturing industry seems to have solved this problem long ago. For example, a car is assembled from many components, most of which are built and tested independently. Nobody waits for the whole car to be ready to test the fuel filter. Some components, sold separately, fit into multiple cars.

Similarly, contract testing and service virtualization are potential solutions to the problems in the IT industry, as they eliminate the need to write complex end-to-end tests and to create independent software components.

Contract Testing

Contract testing is a widely used strategy to test microservices. The contract is an agreement between the producer of the API/message and its consumers. There are two perspectives when it comes to the contract — the consumer and the provider. A consumer is a client who wants to receive some data, and the provider is, for example, an API on a server that provides the data the client seeks. So Google, which provides the Google Maps API, is the *provider* and Uber, which uses it in their app, is the *consumer* of the API.

- *Consumer-driven contract testing*

A consumer-driven contract is a way of formalizing the expectations of the API consumer into a contract. In a traditional setup, the provider is the "boss," and is heedless about the impact on consumers when it makes changes to its APIs. In a consumer-driven approach, however, the consumer makes the contract and the provider ensures the assumptions made in the contract tests are correct.

The consumer-driven approach is not the most effective method for external APIs — where there is little or no communication between consumer and provider. However, it is effective in the development of internal APIs, where collaboration between the provider and consumer teams is possible.

Exhibit 18: Contract testing

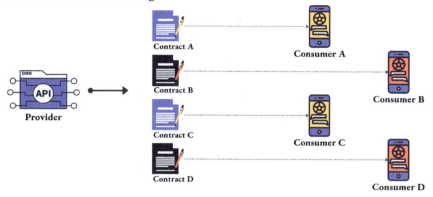

Virtualize Interfaces

Service virtualization is a methodology that simulates services which may not yet be available, may be too costly to implement or simply are not yet developed. While creating digital twins is about virtualizing real-life physical objects, service virtualization focuses on interfaces and interactions between applications and software.

For example, aircraft design and manufacturing is based on a process of continuous simulation, monitoring and improvement. In this way, aircraft building is very different from software development. You cannot wait for and test every environmental condition before an aircraft is ready for production. In fact, simulation is inevitable in a complex environment, be it airlines or the banking industry.

> *"If we built commercial airplanes the same way we build software today, we would never fly!"- John Michelsen, Jason English, "Service Virtualization: Reality Is Overrated"*

Service virtualization is helpful for IoT in developing and testing software against realistic scenarios and at scale before the device itself is available for testing.

Service virtualization creates an asset, known as the *virtual service*, which simulates the behavior of a real component, be it a dependent system, service or database. It is crucial that the service be built by capturing and then intelligently automating the behavior of real systems. In fact, the virtual service should resemble the dependent systems so closely and represent it so well that users think they are interacting with the actual system. Creating such a virtual service is an art.

The fundamental process of building virtual services involves three steps.

- *Listen*

With a help of a recording facility (listener), the transactions between systems, integration layers, components, servers, etc. are first recorded. Using a recording facility works best for existing production ready systems where the interface is already available. In case of a new interface, the virtual service is built from scratch using the specification documents. (A virtual service can replace almost any IT asset that your system can trade information with.)

- *Process*

The captured information is then processed into a virtual service model. This model can be further enhanced with parameterization to support multiple requests and responses. This enhancement makes it possible for development teams to test the connectivity with multiple combinations of data.

- *Respond*

The virtual service is now ready to respond to requests with appropriate data just as the real dependent system would. By eliminating the constraints common in connected devices, virtual services enable quality engineers to autonomously test the device in isolation.

Compliance & Device Certification

QA for smart devices is not complete without compliance and certification, which is much easier for software than hardware. Certification is a formal declaration that a device or product complies with the technical standard, regulation or protocol.

Regulatory certification depends on the country where a device is commercialized — the Federal Communications Commission (FCC) for North America, Radio Equipment Directive (RED) for Europe, etc. Getting a "CE" certification is mandatory for marketing and selling IoT products in the EU region.

The cost of compliance and certification is high if done in the later stages of product development. More than 50% of products fail their compliance checks the first time they are submitted for testing. By conducting pre-compliance tests, you can avoid failures and avoid unpleasant surprises. Some test examples follow.

- *Specific absorption rate (SAR) testing*

SAR measures the rate at which energy is absorbed by the human body when exposed to radio frequency (RF) electromagnetic fields. Regulatory bodies have strict guidelines for wireless devices used within 20 cm. of the body.

This begs the question: *How do you run an energy absorption test on humans?* Of course, you need specialized labs for it. SAR uses standardized models of the human head and body filled with liquids that simulate the RF absorption characteristics of different human tissues. The SAR devices are precisely placed in various positions against the dummy body to conduct a series of measurements.

Exhibit 19: Specific absorption rate

- *Electrical safety testing (EST)*

Electrical safety testing evaluates the potential risk of electrical shocks and physical injury to customers when using the company's products. The hi-pot test, or dielectric strength test, is commonly used to ensure electrical safety. It is performed by applying a high voltage potential between the input live wires and ground. The test passes if the measured current does not exceed a certain low threshold (5mA).

- *Electromagnetic compatibility (EMC)*

EMC tests can be a matter of life and death under certain conditions.[68] For example, 583 people died in the biggest disaster in aviation history at the Tenerife airport off Spain when two Boeing 747s collided on a foggy runway in 1977. The suspected primary cause: electromagnetic interference.

Almost all electronic devices generate some kind of unwanted interference. If you look around your house, you will be amazed at the number of electronic devices you own. How much interference do such devices cause? EMC tests verify products' performance and immunity to external disturbances. Special antennas are placed between three and five meters from the device under test to measure electromagnetic radiation.

---

68   *https://www.tuv.com/content-media-files/master-content/services/ products/0162-tuv-rheinland-electromagnetic-compatibility-(emc)/tuv-rheinland- emc-in-action-whitepaper-2.pdf*

CHAPTER 7

TOUCHPOINTS

"Your brand is a story unfolding across all customer touch points." — Jonah Sachs, Storyteller, Author, Designer and Entrepreneur

- - - - - - - - - - - - - - - - -

We've come a long way since the time when the only interaction a business had with its customers was when they walked into the store to buy something. In a world with more devices than humans on earth,[69] today's consumers have a wealth of available business touchpoints. And all these touchpoints are consequential — each moment and every interaction between companies and their customers and prospects is impactful, an opportunity to provide delightful CX … or to blow it. The challenge with offering a range of touchpoints lies in how to deliver the kind of memorable moments your customers expect regardless of channel and device on which the interaction takes place.

😊 Short Bytes

Michael Aldrich invented online shopping in 1979 (see Exhibit 20) by connecting a modified domestic television to a phone line. With the introduction and vast growth of the internet, the potential of online shopping has surged past being a convenience to being a necessity for nearly everyone.

---

[69] *https://www.rcrwireless.com/20200218/internet-of-things/connected-devices-will-be-3x-the-global-population-by-2023-cisco-says*

Exhibit 20: The first online shopping service

According to a report released by KPMG[70], 77% of China's people say online shopping is their "favorite leisure activity," and it has become the national pastime. With more people everywhere using smart devices and demonstrating an ever-increasing appetite for buying things online, opportunities abound for companies to tap touchpoints to provide the right delightful experiences that produce customer loyalty.

Based on our wide experience, the key driver for success at digital companies is their effort to optimize for all channels and devices, including digital and offline stores, web and mobile apps, and paid or earned media. For today's customers, a key definition of luxury is to select products or services they want, when they want them, on the channel they want.

---

70   *https://assets.kpmg/content/dam/kpmg/cn/pdf/en/2017/12/chinas-connected-consumers-the-rise-of-the-millennials.pdf*

Evolution of Channels

"Channels" are customer touchpoints or other means that allow a customer to interact with the company. Looking back 40 years, before social media, smartphones, tablets and smart devices invaded our homes, we see things were simpler when companies had merely a few channels at their disposal. Today's new challenge is to convey a consistent brand message across channels.

- **Single-channel**

In the beginning, the only way customers could interact with the company was one on one — through the physical store. Service and feedback lines were direct and simple in the single-channel setup. Face-to-face interaction, trust and old-fashioned friendliness made providing excellent customer experience relatively straightforward. Those days are gone.

- **Multichannel**

In a multichannel world, customers have numerous choices of channels in which to interact with the company: mobile, internet, physical ("brick and mortar") store, etc. Customers typcially will use different channels for different purposes: using internet banking for money transfers but going into an actual physical bank to apply for a mortgage. Multichannel living has been part of our well-established world for a while.

- **Omnichannel**

The omnichannel approach — which is the world we are now fully entering — is about providing a cohesive, compelling experience across your brand by unifying the user journey regardless of touchpoint or channel. Omni removes boundaries between different sales and marketing channels to create an integrated experience. The very proliferation of devices and gadgets around us demands an effective omnichannel approach, and this kind of experience is rapidly becoming the rule, not the exception.

Exhibit 21: The channel definitions

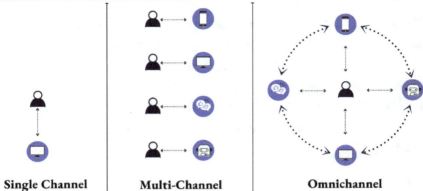

| Single Channel | Multi-Channel | Omnichannel |

Omnichannel Challenges

Omnichannel offers powerfully immersive CX, but implementing it is no easy task. The following challenges often hinder organizations moving toward omnichannel.

- *Lack of holistic view of services*

All too commonly, services are developed in silos within an organization, as they are purpose-built to solve specific problems. Silos are a way of thinking as well as technology structures. Businesses must cultivate a new holistic awareness within employees that removes siloes between departments and encourages them to work collaboratively to maintain top-notch CX. Every employee should have a holistic picture of the product they are building, and the channels on which the customer will use it.

- *Silo effect*

As noted above, silos are isolated and enclosed organizational structures that create artificial barriers between departments, groups, functions, etc. Unfortunately, silos still proliferate at all types and sizes of organizations. According to a research from Bloomfire[71], 40% of the companies say that different departments have their own CX

---

71   https://bloomfire.com/blog/silos-workplace-infographic/

agenda and 41% of CX professionals say that silos pose a significant barrier to providing a seamless experience. Omnichannel, which is a crucial CX enhancer, does not work well with silos. Being a successful omnichannel company requires that internal silos are broken down and eliminated, in order to integrate business processes and data flows across all channel types.

- ***Inventory visibility & metrics***

For an omnichannel business, it is crucial to have up-to-the-second inventory data reflected on each channel. Especially in retail, this is imperative to prevent situations where items are promised but cannot be delivered. With omnichannel selling, companies can no longer rely on traditional inventory management and order fulfilment operations.

The primary problem with traditional inventory management is the persistent deviations between digital inventory tallies and actual hand inventory counts. Common reasons behind this are human error during manual inventory counts, items incorrectly located and inefficient returns processing. To have consistent experience across channels, a real-time predictive inventory management system is a necessity.

- ***Disparate technology & tools***

Omnichannel strategy increases complexity in managing technical operations and integrations. Each channel has its own technical stack and tools, which makes communication between the channels highly complicated. When a business switches to omnichannel, adapting and improving legacy infrastructure and tools should be a high priority. Integrating channels and assuring their quality is a considerable up-front investment. Organizations must opt for a modern technology stack that boosts centralized information management, data governance, access management and the customer journey orchestrator software.

- ***Legacy Systems***

Most large (and even some smaller) organizations today contain massive legacy debts in the form of outdated code bases and outmoded hardware architectures. (This issue relates to the silo factor discussed above.) Legacy applications, by their very disparate structures, impede the control and flexibility organizations need to provide omnichannel experiences.

Obviously, replacing all legacy environments and backend systems with an omnichannel stack is prohibitively expensive for most organizations. One less costly option is to add enhancement layers between your legacy and modern systems and then incrementally upgrade your legacy systems. For example, the core functionality of legacy systems can be encapsulated, and new interfaces could be built around it to leverage the app's functionality. Re-hosting, re-platforming and re-architecting are other options to get around the legacy applications.

- *Change adoption*

Inherent in implementing an omnichannel strategy is *organizational transformation* — involving people, process and technology. The success of the omnichannel effort depends on consensus within the company and adequate change management.

Of course, people resist change, especially when it involves adopting and learning new technology and processes — and this applies to customers not just employees. Plan on allocating sufficient training and communicating the potential of omni to all stakeholders.

- *Data across channels*

With an omnichannel system, large amounts of varied data continually stream from multiple sources such as the web, mobile, IoT devices, etc. All these large chunks of data need to be aggregated and analyzed to ensure meaningful flow across channels. Lack of standardization and disparate protocols make it a challenge to maintain data consistency. A positive CX requires that the system captures customer context — data and status — at every stage of the "conversation" and as their customer identifiers change. Asking the same questions to customers at different stages is a potent turnoff that wrecks the quality of CX, so this kind of integration is vital.

Companies moving to omnichannel need to have an enterprise data management (EDM) strategy in place to holistically join the key building blocks of data management. An EDM system maintains and updates data, keeping up with customers as their identifiers change. Maintaining a consistent identity for each consumer across all their online and offline channels drives a seamless experience.

- *Data quality*

According to a report from independent research firm Vanson Bourne, 77% of the IT decision makers don't completely trust the data in their organization.[72] The aging and obsolescence of data caused by factors like people relocating, switching jobs, etc. adds to the problem of data decay. Mandatory compliance and privacy measures preventing the collection of customer information on a frequent basis further dampen efforts to obtain an enriched customer view.

Developing a data hygiene strategy is a good way to maintain accurate data. Establishing and maintaining optimal data quality typically requires data validation, de-duplication, cleansing, standardization and enrichment.

How to Ensure Omnichannel Quality

The pandemic has shown that commerce can happen anywhere and has pushed more channel adoption. According to a 2021 report from McKinsey, B2B customers now regularly use 10 or more channels to interact with suppliers (up from just five in 2016).[73] But many companies are struggling with omnichannel implementation because

---

72   https://www.snaplogic.com/resources/research/state-of-data-management-impact-of-data-distrust
73   https://www.mckinsey.com/business-functions/marketing-and-sales/our-insights/b2b-sales-omnichannel-everywhere-every-time

keeping up with shifting platforms is such a bear.[74] Ensuring integration of channels to provide a seamless experience means continually evolving the technical infrastructure, architecture and customer engagement models.

Taking retail as a prime example, seamlessly integrating online and in-store channels is key to CX. Though customers start their research online, they finish the actual sales process in the store especially for big ticket items (when the "human touch" is sought for reassurance).

Customers are satisfied only when they get the same high-quality online experience in physical stores, and vice versa. Setting up tablets and in-store kiosks to display store inventory is one way of bringing the online experience to the stores.

Some of the biggest challenges in an omnichannel world are the integration and availability of the numerous interfaces and services. Quality assurance across channels means ensuring:

◆ *Customer experience journeys*
◆ *Customer emotional journeys*
◆ *Holistic quality assurance*

Customer Experience Journeys

The *customer experience journey* is the total experience a customer has with a company across various channels from first contact through final sale. The journey comprises a progression of touchpoints that together add up to the CX associated with the product, services and company itself. Understanding in detail the CX journey — what shape it takes and where your customers are at in it at any point — is a critical input for predicting customer behavior.

The very first exposure to your product or service, the first impression, is known as the *zero moment of truth* (a term coined by Google). It

---

74   https://www.prologis.com/what-we-do/resources/omnichannel-logistics-

challenges

is a decision-making moment that happens countless times a day on smartphones, laptops, pads and other connected devices. From zero moment to the completed purchase requires customers engage, on average, three to five touchpoints or channels.[75]

Create Customer Journey Map

The first step toward enhancing CX across channels is to create a detailed map of the customer journey. Once you know on which channels customers spend their time and for what, it is easier to provide the right experiences on the right devices. Creating the customer journey map involves several steps.

- *Create customer personas*

The first step in creating a customer journey map is to have clear objectives and define who your personas are. Each persona can have a specific behavior and characteristics that can influence the interaction and journey with the customer. A journey map provides maximum benefits when the personas are created as close to the real customer as possible.

- *List channels & touchpoints*

Customer interaction can take place through multiple channels and touchpoints. Some touch points can have more impact than others. It is important to prioritize and list the channels that needs to be mapped per persona. After you define the touchpoints, you can then arrange them on your customer journey map to plot emotions and potential challenges.

---

75   https://www.mckinsey.com/business-functions/operations/our-insights/ redefine-the-omnichannel-approach-focus-on-what-truly-matters

Exhibit 22: Impact of customer journey mapping on experience

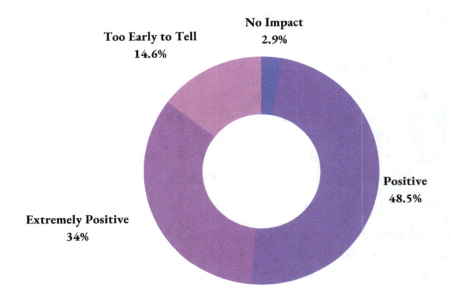

Too Early to Tell
14.6%

No Impact
2.9%

Positive
48.5%

Extremely Positive
34%

Exhibit 23: Customer journey mapping

LUCY, 27 YEARS OLD
Wants to purchase a health insurance policy. Has access to mobile devices and uses social media regularly.

STAGE	AWARENESS	CONSIDERATION	DECISION	SERVICE	LOYALTY
CUSTOMER ACTIONS	Aware: Television & online ads, magazines, social media, websites, chats, word of mouth	Research: Product comparison websites, searches, feedback friends, quotes - price comparison, reviews	Buy the insurance policy	Receive contract and other documentation	Recommend to a friend, take out another policy
TOUCHPOINTS	Websites, media, word of mouth	Websites, over the phone interaction, chats with friends	Mobile app, website, in-person	Contact center, email	Word of mouth, review and rating sites, mobile app, website, in-person
CUSTOMER EXPERIENCE	Interested, hesitant	Curious, excited	Excited	Frustrated	Satisfied
KPIs	Number of people reached	Interest generated	Actual conversion	Customer service successes	Review scores, referrals, number of returning customers
BUSINESS GOALS	Create awareness	Generate interest	Appeal to buy	Delight to use	Wow to recommend

Identify customer pain points

Once the initial customer journey map is done, break down the customer lifecycle into stages such as discovery and research, conversion and post-sale interaction. Plot these stages on the journey map to see where the customer spends the most time, what needs attention and where things go wrong from a quality perspective (for example, the point where customers too frequently abandon their online shopping experience). This exercise should provide enough insight to highlight where to focus your QA efforts in the journey.

- ### Fix roadblocks

  The end goal of creating a journey map is not just to find out where the pain points are but to remove the hurdles and provide an enhanced CX. For example, if your customers' morale is low in the mobile platform where they have to fill in a long form to sign up for services, then the focus should be on creating mobile-friendly forms and further measure how this impacts the journey of the customer. Customers' needs and wishes are evolving constantly and so it is important to keep the journey map up-to-date in finding and resolving new issues.

☺ Short Bytes

#RevengeSpending is a phenomenon of hyperactive consumer spending after some sort of barrier has been removed. The COVID-19 pandemic resulted in an unprecedented adverse economic event causing consumer spending to decline rapidly. People started to save more money and were not able to travel or make any large purchases due to the uncertainty of the situation. As the markets started to open and stabilize, they saw an exponential increase in customer spending on travel, cars, luxury items and even large home renovations. This unsustainable rush to spend by consumers was termed "revenge spending."[76]

---

76   https://timeandtidewatches.com/revenge-spending-will-save-swiss-watch-industry/

Segment Customer Journeys

As your business grows and the customer base increases, your customer journey map becomes more complex to manage. Customer segmentation thus becomes a necessity — to group journeys based on behavior, type of products, time spent on researching, etc. Segmenting helps to run targeted and personalized campaigns to improve experiences.

- *Impulsive journeys*

In *impulsive journeys*, the customer spends less time researching the product and takes buying decisions on the spot, based on visual appeal or previous experiences. A customer buying a perfume, based on a sample and the salesperson's spiel, is an example of an impulsive journey.

- *Balanced journeys*

Balanced journeys are those where the customer starts by making a conscious decision to buy a product or service. They often verify and compare product details against a number of sources across channels and platforms before they arrive at a decision. An example of a balanced journey is where a customer reads online reviews about a product, then gathers feedback from friends and family, walks to a physical store to try the product and finally decides to buy online at the cheapest price.

- *Considered journeys*

Considered journeys kick off with an extended prepurchase period when the customer spends a lot of time researching the product — reading product reviews, news articles and blogs, and gleaning information from friends. This phase helps the customer form an opinion on the product. Considered journeys are usually taken when the customer wants to buy a big-ticket item or something of considerable significance in their life.

For example, a customer who is passionate about cars could spend a lot of time reading up on car features and prices even though he has no immediate need to buy one. When the customer decides to buy, however, buying decisions are driven by the preceding research.

The Emotional Journey

Humans' emotions are constantly in flux, like clouds in the sky. By understanding the peaks and valleys in your customer's emotional journeys, you can identify areas of improvement. Although measuring human emotions can be quite tricky, there are a number of ways to identify emotional states. According to the psychologist and professor Robert Plutchik, there are eight basic emotions: joy, trust, fear, surprise, sadness, anticipation, anger and disgust. These emotions in turn combine, blend, subdivide etc. to form numerous subtler variations.

Plutchik's wheel of emotions (see Exhibit 24 – which is generally presented in full color) provides an excellent framework for understanding customers' emotions and purposes at given points of the buying journey.

Exhibit 24: Plutchik's wheel

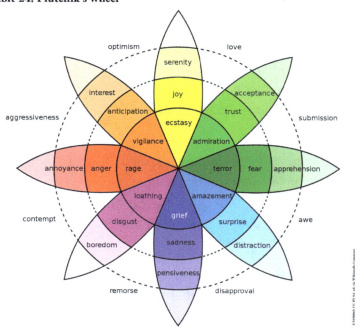

Interpreting the wheel in individual cases requires understanding and analyzing the following three elements.

- **Shades**

Similar emotions are grouped under the same shades.

- **Layers**

Darker colors at the center represent more intense emotions. The layers between emotions, where no colors are shown, represent a mix. For example, a mix of joy and trust results in love.

- **Relationships**

Emotions can also be seen as opposites of each other. For example, joy is the opposite of sadness and trust is the opposite of disgust.

Can human emotions spread like a cold or the flu? The answer is Yes!, and it is known as "emotional contagion."[77] Some research suggests that even indirect relationships, such as those created by social media, can affect emotions. This explains why significant decisions like choosing a leader in an election can be group-influenced by social media.

Assigning scores to Plutchik's wheel allows us to quantify customer emotions. For example, inner-circle emotions can be assigned a score three — plus or minus depending on whether the emotion is positive or negative. The middle circles can have a score of two and the outer circles a score of one.

Assuming in most cases that the customer starts with neutral emotion, or a score of zero, we can score the journey to determine the emotional experience of the customer at any point.

A practical application of using Plutchik's wheel is to classify the feedback and comments that you receive on social media platforms to discern customers' overriding emotions. An example is provided below. This data can be further enhanced to create machine learning models predicting customer emotions (as discussed in the later part of the book).

Emotions	# of comments	Score	Total emotion score
Joy	1234	2	2468
Trust	3256	2	6512
Fear	345	-2	-690
Surprise	500	2	1000
Sadness	123	-2	-246
Disgust	12	-2	-24
Anger	678	-2	-1356
Anticipation	350	2	700

---

77   https://en.wikipedia.org/wiki/Emotional_contagion

Holistic Quality Assurance

It usually takes a number of touchpoints for the customer to be onboarded, nurtured and then converted to be a brand ambassador. *Holistic quality assurance* refers to testing all the individual parts of an application with the bigger picture in mind. This assurance approach is all-encompassing, as it spans channels, technologies, and the realms of software and hardware. Holistic quality assurance does not mean writing large end-to-end (E2E) tests across channels that break often, but rather analyzing all touchpoints to ensure a seamless CX.

Exhibit 25: Channels and usage patterns

Impulsive Buying

Considered Buying

Balanced Buying

Responsive Web Design

Responsive web design is a technique where web pages ask the browser what the device's resolution is, and then the application gracefully redesigns the user experience based on the available screen size. Responsive web pages are fluid, taking whatever shape or size is required. Instead of developers needing to build software for each device, responsive web design creates one variety of software that fits multiple devices.

This is a pressing need. In 2016, the usage of mobile surpassed desktop/laptop users for the first time.[78] Mobility is the new standard, with more than 50% of all internet access taking place through mobile phones.[79] And yet even in 2022 we find a lot of websites that aren't optimized for mobile or tablet.

How can you be sure that your application recognizes the right device and resolution and suitably serves your application to the user? There are dozens of tools in the market to check responsiveness. Simple browser-based tools, like the Chrome developer tools, are a good starting point for basic checks. It is more important to understand *what* to test. The basic checks to ensure responsiveness include the following:

- **Alignment:** *Ensure controls, texts, images etc. are aligned properly.*
- **Clicks:** *Ensure all clickable items on the page, like buttons, links, images, etc. are clickable and do the intended actions.*
- **Loading:** *Check for load speed and performance to ensure there is no drag in any channel.*
- **Fluidity:** *Ensure that text and images fold up nicely or scale well to adapt to device resolution.*

Brand Consistency

One key element of a seamless omnichannel experience is communicating a strong, recognizable, unified brand at all touchpoints. This means visually representing the image, and conveying the same vision and mission, across all channels. Where would Apple be without the bitten apple? McDonalds without their arch? Nike without their swoosh? They are instantly recognizable visual brand legacies. When your brand is consistent, customers develop an emotional bias toward

---

78   https://techcrunch.com/2016/11/01/mobile-internet-use-passes-desktop-for-the-first-time-study-finds
79   https://www.statista.com/statistics/277125/share-of-website-traffic-coming-from-mobile-devices

it through recognition — assuming the other positive CX factors are in place, with their quality assured.

> 😊 **Short Bytes**
>
> *Nike's swoosh logo was designed by Carolyn Davidson,[80] a financially struggling student at Portland State Univ. Pressed by a tight deadline, the company's cofounder, Phil Knight approached Davidson in 1971 to design the logo, telling her just that it needed to have something to do with motion. Davidson produced several concepts, and Knight of course opted for the famous "Swoosh" as Nike's logo. She was paid just $35 ($2 per hour) for this "gig" — creating a logo that eventually became a global icon of a multibillion-dollar corporation. (Happy ending department: Knight later bequeathed Davidson with $1,000,000.)*

One common mistake that companies make is to build identical applications for different touchpoints like the desktop, mobile, tablet, etc. Although visually it gives the impression of a unified, "seamless" experience, in reality customers use different devices in different ways and apps need to reflect that by being tailored to each platform. For example, an application on a mobile device should have less text and larger buttons for higher usability.

It is important to understand the primary objectives each touchpoint is used for. In general, people tend to use their mobile phones for research purposes and turn to their desktop/laptop when actually making the purchase.[81] Even though the volume of mobile users is expanding rapidly, people are still more comfortable making important transactions like major purchases or financial transactions through the desktop application. (The passage of time and widening technology penetration might change this.) Meanwhile, any item added to the

---

80   https://en.wikipedia.org/wiki/Carolyn_Davidson_(graphic_designer)
81   https://www.smartinsights.com/ecommerce/ecommerce-analytics/ecommerce-conversion-rates/

shopping cart via mobile should be available on the full-service website as well, if the customer chooses to make the payment via laptop for example.

Omnichannel works best when a company has integrated its online and offline channels. If for instance the customer's purchase history is known to the employees in a physical store, they can better help the customer straightaway when he enters the store. Linking technology, communication and devices helps move your customer closer to the brand. Basic checks required to ensure brand consistency include the following:

- **Logos & taglines:** *Check for consistent logos and taglines, plus a unified presentation across websites, mobile, social media, ads and other collateral. Though it sounds basic, many companies get it wrong because of devices' varying resolutions.*
- **Visual Testing:** *Always look for visual deformities and resolution inconsistencies.*
- **Translation:** *Don't make the well-known blunder that KFC did when it tried marketing itself in China by translating its tagline "finger lickin' good" to "eat your fingers off."* [82]

---

82   *https://www.businessinsider.com/slogans-that-dont-translate-2013-12*

CHAPTER 8

IMPROVEMENTS

"Measurement is the first step that leads to control and eventually to improvement. If you can't measure something, you can't understand it. If you can't understand it, you can't control it. If you can't control it, you can't improve it."[83] — H. James Harrington, Author, Lecturer, CEO and Quality Guru

----

Kaizen, a Japanese word that stands for *"continuous improvement,"* is well-known in corporate management and consulting circles. In the 1980s, Toyota pioneered the term to help create a culture where all employees are actively engaged in improving the company. Continuous improvement that tracks changing customer desires is an absolute essential, and has been a key factor enabling successful companies with huge customer bases to retain their users.

It is generally expected that companies will update product lines with new products and new features on existing products. In previous eras, the revision timeframe was often annual, but in our digital age improvements are far more frequent – e.g., the many times a month heavily used smartphone apps send updates. But changes are not necessarily improvements, and QA is critical for determining which ones truly satisfy customers' needs and wants. As usual, QA in this area starts with and revolves around measurement. And feedback loops are the first steps to know if you are doing something right or wrong and what your customer really wants and needs.

---

83   *https://www.goodreads.com/author/quotes/42617.H_James_Harrington*

Measure to Improve

One danger of possessing knowledge is the cognitive bias that can occur when an individual, in communicating with other individuals, unknowingly assumes that others have the background knowledge to understand. This happens often in the technology industry, where developers assume a certain level of expertise to use their products. Many times in such scenarios, comments from customers concerning usability are ignored or downplayed, even though their customers' technical competence levels should help guide development efforts.

Paying careful attention to customer feedback can help an organization break (or avoid) this curse, by understanding the product from their customers' perspectives and making the indicated changes to improve usability and hence CX.

Analyzing feedback data is how we learn, and how we stay motivated. As human psychology tells us, by focusing on a particular metric every single day, we are likely to improve on it.[84] A perfect example is the success of devices like Fitbit and other smartwatches that constantly feed users with information like number of steps, distance, calories burned, etc. The numbers motivate people to improve and perform better to improve their statistics.

How to Measure Experiences

Traditional quality test metrics like defect density, defect leakage, test coverage, etc. still play a role in the quality field, but these metrics are mostly output based and do not measure outcomes. The metrics that matter most are those that measure how satisfied your customers are.

In the digital world, we have evolved meaningful metrics that help solve the deeper challenges of experience and satisfaction. We'll look at the most commonly used feedback collection mechanisms:

---

84   https://www.psychologytoday.com/us/blog/glue/202107/how-benefit-the-scoreboard-principle

◆*Overall satisfaction*
◆*Net promoter score*
◆*Customer effort score*
◆*Customer lifetime value*
◆*Customer health score*
◆ *Customer retention rate*
◆ *Mean opinion score*
◆ *Google's HEART framework*

Overall Satisfaction (OSAT)

As the name makes clear, *overall satisfaction (SAT)* captures the total satisfaction of the customer. Its basis is the collective answers to the customer survey question, *"How likely are you to refer our products or services to a friend or colleague?"* Customers are asked to provide feedback usually in the Likert scale — a psychometric scale commonly used in questionnaires that registers responses usually in the range of 0 to 5, 7 or 10 points.

At what point in a customer survey should the OSAT question be asked is debatable, with different experts holding varying opinions. Asking it right at the beginning of the questionnaire has the advantages of capturing customers' spontaneous, unbiased opinion. Making it the last question in the survey, however, gives customers time to have thought through the previous questions, and so might better represent their considered opinion. So while there is no right or wrong place to place OSAT questions, it is important to be aware that its placement will have an impact on the results.

Net Promoter Score (NPS)

The *net promoter score* is an index ranging from -100 to +100 that measures customers' willingness to recommend a company's products or services to others. NPS is calculated by dividing customers into three categories: promoters, detractors and passives. This classification is based on how they scored the OSAT question, say on a scale of 1 to

10. Your NPS is the difference between the percentage of promoters and the percentage of detractors.

- **Detractors**

Detractors are your unhappy customers. Detractors can damage your brand reputation, spread negativity and harm your business. They use social media, discussion forums, etc. Typically, these people rate their satisfaction at 0 to 6.

- **Passives**

Passives are satisfied and may not complain about your product or services, but they are not strongly opinionated and can be lured by competitors or distracted by competitive offers from other companies. Typically, these people rate their satisfaction at 7 to 8.

- **Promoters**

Promoters are highly satisfied, loyal customers who are very enthusiastic about the product. They help build brand reputation and can become evangelists of your products or services. Typically, these people rate their satisfaction at 9 to 10.

Exhibit 26: Promoters, passives and detractors

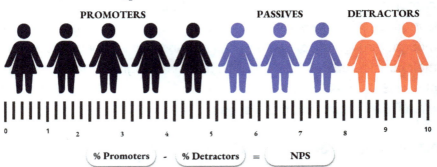

The first documented customer service complaint is from 1750 BC when a customer named Nanni received a shipment of copper ore from the merchant Ea-nasir in ancient Ur.[85] The quality of ore that was eventually received was inferior to what was expected, and there had been other annoying delays in the supply. The complaint was inscribed in a clay tablet, written in Akkadian cuneiform, *which is now housed at the British Museum.*

Exhibit 27: The first customer complaint inscribed in a clay tablet

Customer Effort Score (CES)

The *customer effort score* measures how much energy is required by a customer to complete a particular task. Research shows that the ease of a given experience correlates even more closely with customer loyalty than customer satisfaction.[86]

Examples of excessive effort to engage with a product include making a customer switch channels to complete a transaction or forcing them to repeat themselves multiple times to explain a product issue. Such increased efforts result in lower customer satisfaction and degraded CX.

---

85   https://en.wikipedia.org/wiki/Complaint_tablet_to_Ea-nasir
86   https://www.gartner.com/smarterwithgartner/effortless-experience-explained

Measuring CES is easily done by asking a simple question after a product purchase or transaction:

To what extent do you agree to the below statement?

Buying a product through our website was easy and handy.

1. *Strongly agree*
2. *Agree*
3. *Somewhat agree*
4. *Somewhat disagree*
5. *Disagree*
6. *Strongly disagree*

Most companies generally send out a CES survey after a touchpoint interaction with customer service or after a customer has reported an issue. However, development teams are now more widely using CES to assess the ease of use of new features and to identify where and when customers begin to feel frustrated and lost.

Customer Lifetime Value (CLV)

Customer lifetime value (CLV) is, as its name indicates, the total worth of a customer to a business over the whole period of their relationship. In other words, CLV is the projected revenue that a customer will generate over their lifetime.

> 😃 Short Bytes
>
> *What do you think is the CLV of an average Starbuck's coffee drinker?* To answer that question, one must know the average lifespan of a customer at Starbucks. The average time someone remains a customer at Starbucks is about 20 years. According to some calculations, the CLV of an average Starbucks customer is about $14,099.[87]

---

87   *https://www.visualcapitalist.com/calculating-lifetime-customer-value/*

In simple terms, *CLV is the customer revenue minus the cost of acquiring and serving the customer.*

Because CLV is directly linked to revenue, it is distinct from NPS and CSAT. Measuring CLV provides an opportunity to improve revenue by improving customer satisfaction — which leads to greater per-visit spends — and loyalty — which keeps the money flowing.

> ☺ Short Bytes
>
> *As of 2021, Netflix had about 214 million paid memberships globally.[88] The average Netflix subscriber stays on board for 25 months. According to Netflix, the lifetime value of a Netflix customer is $291.25. This figure helps Netflix calculate how much they should spend per customer on marketing and overhead.*

Customer Health Score (CHS)

The *Customer health score* consolidates all sources of information about a customer by taking several customer data metrics such as CES and NPS and visualizing them in a simple traffic-light model: green/amber/red. A green designation means the customer is getting value from the products, services and interactions with the company. Amber indicates that the customer is currently satisfied but inattention would result in a deterioration of loyalty and a drift into the red zone. Red means that something is not going well for the customer, which is likely to lead to churn: Perhaps one or more interactions of the customer hadn't gone well at a touchpoint. The key to mending the relationship is to proactively reach out to the customer with a recovery plan. Thus, the customer health score is also akin to an early warning system to target customers who require attention.

---

88   *https://www.insiderintelligence.com/insights/netflix-subscribers/*

Exhibit 28: Customer health score

		CURRENT STATE	ACTION TO TAKE
🙂	DOING WELL	The customer is doing well and seems satisfied with the service	Continue nurturing the customer to establish loyalty
😐	TAKE NOTICE	The customer is somewhere in between. If left unchecked they might deteriorate to poor health	Monitor the customer closely and provide required attention
😠	NEEDS ATTENTION	The customer is not doing well. If left unchecked will likely unsubscribe	Make a well defined plan to restore customer trust

Customer Retention Rate (CRR)

The *customer retention rate* (CRR) designates the percentage of customers the company has retained over a period of time. According to a classic *Harvard Business Review* article. acquiring a new customer is between five and 25 times more expensive than retaining an existing one.[89]

The formula for deriving this value is quite simple:

Customer retention rate =

(# Customers at End of Period - # Customers Acquired During Period) / # Customers at Start of Period x 100

Obviously, businesses are always on the lookout for new customers, but smart companies also understand that building an empire means not just adding new customers but retaining loyal existing ones. The harsh truth is that the customer retention rate in many industries is less than 50% today,[90] indicating that it is time for companies

---

89   https://hbr.org/2014/10/the-value-of-keeping-the-right-customers
90   https://surveysparrow.com/blog/heres-something-didnt-know-average-customer-retention-rate-industry/

to dedicate the time, resources and money to focus on retaining customers. Creating customer loyalty programs, personalizing customers' journeys and offering incentives for returning customers are top ways to improve CRR.

Mean Opinion Score (MOS)

The *mean opinion score (MOS)* numerically measures human perception of the overall quality of an event or experience. MOS is widely used in the telecommunications industry to rank the quality of voice and video sessions. In telephonic interactions, voice quality determines whether the experience is good or bad. The MOS score is determined by human evaluators sitting in a "quiet room" where they score call quality on a scale from one (worst) to five (best). The average, or the arithmetic mean, of all the individual scores is the MOS value.

Google's HEART Framework

Collecting metrics through feedback questionnaires, surveys, rating mechanism, etc. works well at a small scale, but collecting click paths and usage metrics manually is not practical on a larger scale.

A remedy to this problem emerged when Google's Kerry Rodden, Hilary Hutchinson and Xin Fu designed the HEART framework to measure user experience at a large scale. They found that with the huge amount of data Google collected, it is essential to scope out what to look for and analyze. They categorized the metrics into five buckets: Happiness, Engagement, Adoption, Retention and Task success.

- *Happiness*

This measure refers to the subjective aspects of CX such as satisfaction, visual appeal, likelihood to recommend and perceived ease of use. It offers a heuristic on how your customers feel about your product or service.

- **Engagement**

This describes the behavioral aspects of experience such as frequency of interaction, depth of interaction over time, duration of activity, etc.

- **Adoption**

This metric captures the number of new customers onboarded in a given period. It provides a strong indication of how well the product or feature is received by the customers.

- **Retention**

This metric, which captures the count of returning customers in a given period, is an excellent measure of customer loyalty.

- **Task success**

This measures how efficiently and effectively a user can complete a task. Factors such as how long it takes a user to complete a task, errors encountered, usability, etc. are grouped under this umbrella.

Exhibit 29: Google heart framework

	Goals	Signals	Metrics
HAPPINESS	Customers find the app helpful, fun and easy to use	Leaving good feedback, 5-star ratings and responding to surveys	Increase in NPS Customer satisfaction score
ENGAGEMENT	Customers enjoy the app and keep engaging with it	Customers engaging for longer time than usual	Average session length and conversion time
ADOPTION	New customers see the value of the app and it's features	Downloading new version of app, adopting features, signing up	Download and new registrations rate
RETENTION	Customers are loyal and keep coming back to use the app	Renewing subscription and making repeat purchases	Churn rate Subscription renewal date
TASK SUCCESS	Customers are able to complete their goals quickly and easily	Completing tasks quickly and efficiently	Search exit rate Crash rate

How to Improve Experiences

While listening to customers and measuring their responses is vital, customers will only get more frustrated if you fail to act on the feedback collected. And asking for *further* feedback before acting on *previously collected* responses will only make that frustration worse. To counter that, the following six directives will directly enhance CX.

- **Act on time**

It's always discouraging when disgruntled customers or others point out bugs and other flaws in a product or service you have spent months or years to perfect. The inclination is to move slowly. But critical comments from customers require immediate action to avoid customer churn. Feedback heard from many users should carry a lot of weight, as those issues are highly relevant.

- **Be agile**

Managing CX is not a onetime activity but a continuous, consistent process. Make it a habit to prioritize and pick up at least a couple of customer feedback stories during each Sprint. Customer satisfaction shifts and changes over time, so monitoring feedback and incorporating changes with agility should help ensure that customer satisfaction never falls below an acceptable level.

- **Tell your customers**

Tell your customers that you listened, because "communication is king." Email back to your customers about how their feedback helped you to enhance the product, feature or service. It is deeply satisfying for a customer to hear that their comments were valuable and the company has acted on them. Not only are they encouraged to provide additional timely feedback, but such responsiveness also likely makes them a "brand ambassador."

- **Be digitally inclusive**

Digital inclusion refers to the activities necessary to ensure that all individuals and communities including the most disadvantaged have access to and use of technologies. Today, 4.66 billion people[91] have

---

91   *https://www.statista.com/statistics/617136/digital-population-worldwide/#:~:text=How%20many%20people%20use%20the,the%20internet%20via%20mobile%20devices.*

some access to the internet, which has been the driving force behind the digital revolution. The digital boom will continue to grow, or even accelerate. Technology is shaping every walk of life including day-to-day tasks like buying groceries.[92]

> Q: What if someone does not want to change? What happens if someone is not connected to the connected world?

> A: They will be left behind.

According to a survey in England[93], around 12% of the population will lack basic digital literacy within a decade. The adoption of new technology threatens their ability to pay bills, contact banks, book flights, renew passports and check their benefits.

- **Design for disability**

With 15% of the world's population living with some form of disability[94], representing over $13 trillion in annual disposable income,[95] it is a serious oversight to ignore disability in CX. So designing for disability is not only humane, but profitable. And as populations age, the incidence of disabilities increases; the population of Americans over 65 years old is expected to nearly double in the coming three decades. Americans with Disabilities Act (ADA) standards for accessible design requires companies to ensure that people with disabilities can use and access their sites.[96] A 2019 Click-Away-Pound survey revealed that approximately 7.15 million UK residents have access needs, and their estimated spending power is £24.8. billion.[97]

---

92   https://www.foodlogistics.com/software-technology/software-solutions/ article/21271093/bazaarvoice-technology-changes-how-we-grocery-shop

93   https://www.telegraph.co.uk/technology/2018/09/11/lack-digital-skills-will-leave-7-million-left-behind-next-decade/

94   https://www.who.int/news-room/fact-sheets/detail/disability-and-health

95   https://www.rod-group.com/content/rod-research/edit-research-design-delight-disability-2020-annual-report-global-economics

96   https://www.ada.gov/2010ADAstandards_index.htm

97   http://www.clickawaypound.com/downloads/cap19final0502.pdf

Most significantly, 69% of disabled customers with access needs say they click away from a website they find it difficult to use, and 86% of such customers say they would spend more if websites were more accessible.[98]

Adhering to the new Web Content Accessibility Guidelines (WCAG) is an excellent start, as they provide recommendations for designers to make web content (text, images and sounds, on various devices) more accessible for people with disabilities.

With digital innovations rising, design innovations are badly needed to improve accessibility in an inclusive digital experience. One example of such innovation is VoiceOver.

☺ Short Bytes

The smartphone's touch screen is a de facto standard, whose advent was a revolutionary development. The question was, how will visually impaired individuals access the phone? To solve this, Apple came up with the "VoiceOver," the world's first gesture-based screen reader. VoiceOver on iOS interacts with the user by using various "gestures" — motions the user makes with one or more fingers on the display.

- **Co-browse**

The *co-browsing* technique allows people to collaboratively browse a website or app in real time. For example, service agents in contact centers commonly use co-browsing to understand and solve customers' problems. Co-browsing sends the agent an accurate visual representation of the customer's view of the website. Physically guiding customers who are frustrated or confused not only helps resolve their issue but also provides the necessary learning for them to be able to do it themselves in the future. It is a great tool for reducing customer effort and improving CES. Of course, there are security concerns

---

98   http://www.clickawaypound.com/downloads/cap19final0502.pdf

when sensitive data is being displayed. Properly obfuscating such information in the agent's view and asking explicit permission from the customer to access the browsers are ways to mitigate it.

Experiences that "WOW"

WHAT 'WOWS' CUSTOMERS

Merely doing a "satisfying" or "good" job doesn't cut it anymore. Such mildly positive experiences do not help create guarantee customer loyalty. To achieve the lofty goal of brand loyalty requires a business to far exceed users' expectations, to go past appealing or delightful experiences, and achieve a "Wow!" response. This "wow factor" keeps customers coming back, and establishes a powerful loyalty to the brand — the ultimate business goal.

In the past, such "wow" experiences were created solely by people. Even though processes, policies, and practices did greatly influence CX, the elements that created truly memorable moments were usually generated by an employee who went out of the way to ensure that a customer was happy, helped out a customer in distress or even made an exception to satisfy a customer's needs. These moments of service sealed the deal in their way, forging long-term bonds between customer and company.

The game, however, has changed drastically in our era; old-fashioned service won't go out of style, but we've moved beyond the stage when an employee's intervention is the chief way to deeply impress customers. We now see that *technology is the new driving force for producing the wow response*, as advances in machine learning and other varieties of AI have changed virtually everything.

AI's capabilities include the ability to "know" a customer — predict their behavior, anticipate their needs and provide round-the-clock support. These abilities are perfectly suited to enhancing and enriching CX, and creating wow effects consistently and often. In fact, CX practitioners were among the earliest adopters of AI, seeing its opportunities before many others did. They saw that AI's 24-hours-a-day availability, ability to extract meaning from data and mind-boggling speed of action make it possible to provide personalized services for every single customer. Such customization has become the new frontier in CX, the land of the wow experience.

CHAPTER 9

PREDICTION

"I set the date for the Singularity—representing a profound and disruptive transformation in human capability—as 2045. The nonbiological intelligence created in that year will be one billion times more powerful than all human intelligence today."
— *Ray Kurzweil, Author, Inventor*

- - - - - - - - - - - - - - - - -

In the never-ending drive for business success, the ability to know what customers are likely to do next is obviously a huge advantage which every company would love to have. Predicting customers' behavior is crucial for companies to conduct targeted marketing and make product recommendations. It also confers clear benefits for cybersecurity.

However, creating such an effect of virtual *clairvoyance* (perceiving things or events in the future or beyond normal sensory contact) demands companies deploy near-"supernatural" powers. The name of these powers? *Modern data analytics*. These allow company to predict the future by intricately parsing the past and present. For example, by tracking a customer's search patterns, click paths, page views and related metrics, a company can predict with astonishing accuracy the customer's buying patterns and most suitable products.

Some applications fitted with predictive behavioral analytics draw on an organization's accumulated user data to peg visitors as impulsive purchasers, researchers or order-cancellers. The beauty of these algorithms is that they are instantaneous and improve as more data accumulates.

Take the example of grocery substitution. When people buy online and there are stockouts, the pickers select substitutes, which are often "wrong" for the given customer — a clearly negative impact on CX. Walmart has solved this problem with behavioral data and AI to predict the behavior of the customer and the choices they would make in case a particular item is out of stock. With this technology. Walmart's has increased customer acceptance of substitutions to over 95%.[99]

Exhibit 30: Customer behaviour prediction

Another example is Amazon's anticipatory shipping before the customer has even placed an order. Pairing predictive analytics tools with its trove of customer data, Amazon can predict purchasing behavior and make shipments to the nearest warehouse to reduce fulfilment time.

This is the new world of data-driven marketing and experience assurance. With unprecedented reams of data available for predicting customer behavior, companies need to segment, analyze and process this information to fully understand their customers on a granular level.

Predicting Behavior With AI

Artificial intelligence (AI), the area of computer science behind the creation of intelligent machines that work and react like humans, has

99   https://corporate.walmart.com/newsroom/2021/06/24/headline-how-walmart-is-using-a-i-to-make-smarter-substitutions-in-online-grocery-orders

actually been around a while. Few realize that from a hand calculator to the autopilots used by the aviation industry, AI has long been part of our technical culture. But in recent years, AI implementations have soared, triggered by advancements in areas of AI like machine learning (ML), natural language processing (NLP), deep learning, etc.

Knowing when your customer interacts with the application or makes a purchase is an important input in predicting customer behavior. There are universal occasions like Black Friday, the Christmas shopping season, etc. where people tend to buy more. And there are unique occasions that are personal to a customer: birthdays, anniversaries, etc.

Companies like Starbucks[100] leverage information about customers' buying patterns to target them. Starbucks has enough data from a variety of sources like transactions, loyalty programs, product and store information to predict the behavior of a customer — when, for instance, the customer is more likely to buy a muffin in addition to a coffee. This helps Starbucks to target appropriate personalized offers to customers on the right days to encourage more buying behavior. Adding extra dimensions to this data analysis such as weather conditions can create magic by providing wow experiences, thanks to AI. Predicting behavior with AI involves the following steps and challenges.

100   https://formation.ai/blog/how-starbucks-became-1-in-customer-loyalty/

Predicting human behavior and emotions is a tough job and even more for a machine. How cool will it be for machines to understand our emotions and work collaboratively with us? Columbia Engineering researchers have taken a significant step in that direction by developing a computer vision algorithm to predict human interactions and body language.[101] The algorithm was trained on thousands of hours of movies, sports and popular TV shows like The Office *to understand human emotions and predict what the next action would be — hug, kiss, cry, etc.*

- ### Data gathering & processing

The first step in AI-based prediction is to define the data required and gather it from different sources. Usually, segmented data with related attributes provides better results for processing. Customer behavior data is available in the form of historic transactions, click paths, search histories, feedback comments, surveys, influence factors, data entries, etc. All of these are potential inputs.

- ### Filtering noise in data

Noise, or meaningless data, is detrimental to data analytics. Typical data errors are often due to the misuse of abbreviations, mis-filled-in words, data entry mistakes, duplicate records, missing values, spelling errors, outdated codes, etc. In addition to data cleansing, removing outliers is a great way to filter noise in data. Outliers are extreme values that deviate from other data which might indicate a faulty measurement, experimental error or a novelty that can be safely ignored. However, the golden rule of data processing is to not meddle with the source data so much that the results do not fully represent the data. Finding the balance is crucial.

---

101   *https://www.engineering.columbia.edu/press-release/ai-learns-to-predict-human-behavior-from-videos*

- **Data splitting**

The next step in data processing is to split the data into training and test data sets. The split is usually 70% of the data for training purposes and 30% of data for testing purposes. Training data sets are data sets of examples from history used to teach the ML algorithm, based on which model is being built. The testing data set is used to measure the accuracy of the model.

- **Choosing an algorithm**

Choosing the right algorithm for the right data is the biggest challenge in setting up an ML-based prediction model. Selecting an algorithm for a particular use case is influenced by a number of factors: accuracy, training effort and infrastructure availability.

Accuracy: Choosing an algorithm that can predict most accurately sounds obvious, but in reality, accuracy is not an absolute measure for such choosing. For example, if you are building a ML model to predict the outcome of flight landing, you are already starting with imbalanced historical data because the percentage of successful landing is more than 99%. So even when the model fails to predict a crash, its accuracy technically is still more than 99%.

The more an algorithm is trained on a specific set of data, the more accurate it becomes. When exposed to a different set of data, however, the accuracy changes and the model needs more training to get good prediction accuracy.

Training effort: The time required to train a good prediction model varies significantly with the type of algorithm chosen. Some algorithms work best with larger data sets, and some get good accuracy with limited data sets. Bayesian methods work best with small datasets in creating simple regression and classification models. For image processing and AI vision, a large dataset is usually required to get the right level of accuracy in the output. When time is limited, the effort required to train a model can drive the choice for the algorithm.

Infrastructure availability: Many ML models are data- and process-intensive, so the choice of algorithm could be contingent on how much processing capacity and memory resources are available. Central processing units (CPUs) are suitable for most machine learning models and to run complex calculations sequentially. Graphics processing units (GPUs) are required to run parallel executions of deep learning models and visual image processing.

- **Evaluating the model**

Evaluating the ML model is an essential part of the process. After the model is trained, the test data set is used to validate it. The accuracy of the model to predict behavior is measured, and based on the results further fine tuning is conducted.

- **Predicting**

Prediction, or inference, is the step where the value of ML is fully realized. This is when new data is fed to the model to make predictions on behaviors.

Risks of AI-Assisted Prediction

Predicting customer behavior is a risky undertaking, with a big upside but a potentially damaging downside if predictions are off base. Risks associated with AI-assisted prediction fall into three categories: data, algorithmic and learning.

- **Data risks**

With ML effectiveness so dependent on data, the failure to harness it properly can trigger huge failures. Hence, your quality assurance strategy should be focused on mitigating data-related issues.

First, historic data collected to train the model should completely represent the use case and the environment in which AI operates. An ML model that does not fully represent the data can quickly become irrelevant, even though it had been fully relevant in the past.

Good sampling and representation of data does not mean that the data is good for ML or deep learning algorithms. Raw historic data can lead to biases. For example, in a company with predominantly male employees, using employee data would lead to an obvious gender bias. The infamous AI-based app made by Amazon[102] that rejected all female candidates applying for a job because it was trained with more male candidate resumés is one of the biggest AI failures in recent times.

- *Algorithmic risks*

Matching the algorithm correctly for the data at hand is a critical challenge. With many packaged plug-and-play algorithms available in the market, there is a risk of using it in ways they were not designed for or of facing issues if the algorithms have not been defined properly. Programmers use most algorithms as "black boxes," so even an algorithm that offers a high level of accuracy has not necessarily learned the right things or can predict what is required. The lack of visualization and users' inability to explain the nature of an algorithm means there could be potential points of failure embedded within the algorithm.

- *Learning risks*

Algorithms are highly "impressionable." As the model continuously learns from new data, it is impossible to determine who is responsible for any harm that may arise with incorrect predictions or inappropriate interactions. If users continuously ask inappropriate questions, the self-learning models try to predict an answer that doesn't exist and could soon turn out to be wildly inaccurate. Lack of any regulations at the moment means there are no clear guidelines on who could be held responsible for what.

---

102   *https://www.reuters.com/article/us-amazon-com-jobs-automation-insight-idUSKCN1MK08G*

With sufficient malicious input, an algorithm can be misled to do things it was not designed for. For example, Microsoft's chatbot Tay developed racial biases due to mislearning.[103]

Using Behavior Prediction to Ensure Quality

Predicting a specific customer's behavior in order to personalize CX offers distinct competitive advantage. The flipside is that a *wrong* prediction is worse than making no prediction at all. How many times have you seen irrelevant ads and personalized offers that don't match your expectations? Deriving the right insights and recommendations and thoughtfully delivering exactly what customers need for a personalized experience involves several steps:

◆ *Segmenting customer behavior*
◆ *Understanding customer sentiment*
◆ *Monitoring synthetic & real users*
◆ *Ensuring the right level of personalization*

Segmenting Customer Behavior

Customer segmentation is dividing them into groups of similar individuals based on various selected criteria: age, sex, demographics, interests, browsing patterns, purchasing history, etc. It's a powerful analytical and prescriptive tool for predicting customer behavior and providing them with "right-fit" services at the right times. Segmentation has been used for decades, but especially now that CX and personalization are make-or-break issues for businesses, it is an absolute must. Segmenting approaches can range from manual human judgment to advanced clustering techniques using ML. For simple classification of customers based on one or two criteria, human judgement is probably sufficient. But when it comes to huge volumes of data and combining multiple criteria — like relating the click-path-behavior of customers with demographic data — advanced ML algorithms are required.

---

103   https://en.wikipedia.org/wiki/Tay_(bot)

A key subset of customer segmentation is behavioral segmentation, which classifies the customer population based on specific behavioral patterns they display while interacting with the product or service. The behavior in question can range widely: It could be a "conversion event" like a purchase decision, or a particular way of using the application, choices of features, etc. Creating such segments enables a company to understand how users interact with its application, what makes them convert and, most importantly, where CX can be improved. There are numerous ways to segment customers based on behavior. Purchasing patterns and click path behavior are perhaps the most common buckets.

- **Purchase behavior**

One primary and obvious reason to segment customers based on purchase history is to send appropriately targeted marketing messages and ads. We all know how that works. For example, this is why Amazon places so much emphasis on the past purchase history of its customers to provide suggestions for future purchases.

- **Click path behavior**

Segmenting customers based on their click path history helps to identify patterns of browsing and other actions, and thereby conduct targeted outreach. Clicks and engagement data provide reams of information on peoples' interests, motivations, patterns, etc. Today's powerful analytical apps facilitate such granular explorations and enable actionable insights. For example, a user might hit your website frequently to explore a product or two and also check the FAQ page — without ever making a purchase. Their behavior clearly shows interest in the products but also that there is an impediment to completing the purchase. Such information about their search parameters helps guide the most effective way to reach out to such a customer with relevant information or offers.

Understanding Customer Sentiment

Sentiment analysis is a contextual mining technique where a piece of written text is analyzed to determine if its tone is positive, negative or neutral. The most important indicators are the sentiment words, also called opinion words. Sentiment is crucial in the world of voice and choice, as it offers valuable insights on CX — what customers like and dislike about the product, services, branding, etc.

As we all know, opinions are key influencers of human behavior. Customers' opinions about your products and services determine their degree of loyalty and the type of peer recommendations they make. In recent years, we have seen the great impact that opinionated social media posts can have on businesses and even elections.

Unlike objective facts, opinions, feedback and related sentiments are subjective, and subject to change. So sentiment analysis is not merely a one-time activity, but an ongoing pursuit. Reviewing customer feedback regularly enables businesses to deploy proactive measures based on market dynamics. It is also important to consider the feedback of multiple people to counterbalance the effects of subjectivity.

Gathering Customer Sentiment

- ***Social media channels***

In our digital world, social media is a key channel from which to collect customer feedback. With 4.55 billion social media users in 2021,[104] customer feedback potentially can have a profound influence on existing and future customers. This is where customers are doing much of their talking about your brand and products, so wise companies pay close attention to what is being said and show they are really listening by responding to online feedback. It might sound obvious, but customer participation is driven by knowing they are being heard. Provide fair and suitable replies to the feedback that customers leave even if it means sometimes you need to admit your mistakes.

---

104   *https://datareportal.com/reports/digital-2021-october-global-statshot*

- ***Direct customer feedback***

Sometimes the best way to glean a customer's response is to ask them directly. The highest rung of making a customer feel privileged is to ask for feedback face to face. But that is possible only in the physical store channel, and besides, sometimes people are not direct or even truthful about their opinions when faced with an unexpected query about their response.

Sending direct personal emails to customers with a touch of personalization is a good approach for getting reasonably candid feedback. Unlike in social channels, the direct feedback responses are not seen by other users, and this opens the door for customers and companies to engage in interesting conversations.

- ***Surveys***

Another common measure is the old-fashioned customer survey, now delivered electronically most of the time. Customers should be able to choose whether their survey responses will be anonymous or personalized feedback. The big challenge in surveys is to get customers to participate.

When sending any survey, always mention how long it will likely take to complete. After all, customers want their time to be valued and so this reduces the number of people who drop out partway through the survey. A sharp statement on what the company intends to do with the feedback can also be a good motivator for participation. For businesses like hotel booking sites or vacation providers, these survey results when publicly available helps a customer to make decisions that can build or burn a business.

- ***App stores***

Ratings and reviews on app stores not only indicate the quality of CX but also help other customers decide whether to use the app or not. It is impossible to satisfy all the customers no matter how good your app is. Some customers will simply have different expectations, and also a lack of knowledge could trigger negative feedback. Negative feedback needs to be addressed promptly and deftly to avoid customer churn. Politely explaining why the product did not work as they expected will not only increase the customer's confidence in the company, it will encourage others to provide candid feedback.

- **Customer service logs**

Text logs in live chat can be used not only for quality control of the support but also to identify what customers are saying about products and services, and what issues they are encountering.

Monitoring Synthetic & Real Users

Synthetic testing is a method of understanding a user›s experience of your application by predicting behavior. Synthetic testing tools employ simulated users to provide information on uptime, the performance of critical business transactions and most common navigation paths. The aim is to predict what your customers would consume next and make sure the desired functionality is available for the customer.

- **Browser monitor**

Browser monitors are emulations of an actual customer using your application. The user's behavior is emulated by either using the URLs or click paths. Once you have captured all actions that you want to monitor through click paths, automatic runs can be set up to monitor site functionality and performance. Browser monitors alert you when your application is unavailable or the baseline performance degrades.

- **Ping monitor**

The simplest form of synthetic monitoring, a *ping monitor* merely checks if an application is online. Ping monitors run at regular intervals to check if your website or API is available by pinging the endpoints.

- **API monitor**

API monitors are simple API requests to check if your website or API endpoint is available. API monitors check the availability of services in the sequence of simulated user behavior.

Real User Monitoring (RUM)

Real user monitoring and synthetic testing are complementary. In contrast to synthetic testing, RUM measures users' actual experiences as they interact with applications. RUM technology collects a website or app's performance data directly from the end user's browser. It embeds a simple JavaScript on each page to monitor user actions and transfers the data back for analysis. The most well-known example of RUM is Google Analytics, which tracks certain types of interaction between users and the website, like page views, click paths, browser history and traffic sources.

- **Data collection**

Here, a code snippet placed in the web page constantly sends user behavior information like click paths, data entry, page load times, failures, timeouts, etc. The collected data is aggregated and segmented based on user segments, browsers and components.

- **Data analysis**

Collected data is then analyzed for unusual behavior such as page abandonment, slow response times, navigation errors, broken links and other malfunctions. The analysis aims to recreate every individual customer experience, especially when things go wrong. Using the data collected and analyzed in real time, it is possible to reduce bottlenecks, decrease issues, and delight or wow customers with rapid resolution of issues.

- **Reporting & alerting**

Reports on the real-time customer experience are sent to all stakeholders through dashboards and custom-made documents.

The report summarizes the aggregated data, which can be further drilled into to obtain details on a particular page or content. When an issue is detected, an alert mechanism reports the issue to support specialists who can resolve it.

Ensuring the Right Level of Personalization

Personalization consists of tailoring a service or a product to accommodate specific individuals or segments of individuals to improve their satisfaction and CX. In other words, personalization is a matchmaking exercise between what your customer needs and what your product offers them. Segmenting customers and knowing where exactly the customer is in the journey helps to provide personalized services.

The best customer experiences are consistently personal. Take your name, which is a highly personal thing. Imagine having a Coke with your name printed on it. In the "Share a Coke" campaign, Coca-Cola printed the most common names on Coke bottles to attract more millennials. With this simple marketing strategy, they built stronger and more personal relationships with customers while increasing sales. Personalization not only connects with customers, it is a great way to empower them to find or do what they want — thereby increasing sales.

Exhibit 31: Levels of personalization

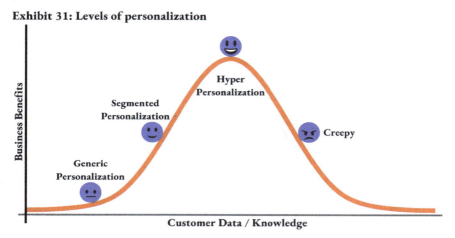

- ***Generic personalization***

Do you remember the nice email that you got on your birthday from the store where you bought your shoes? It is a great way for companies to say that they care about their customers and can also drive traffic to their website.

However, it no longer stands out from an experience perspective as everybody understands those are auto generated emails with standard texts. Generic personalization is done based on raw customer data and has the ability to trigger simple positive experiences.

- ***Segmented personalization***

By segmenting groups of customers via behaviors, traits, personas or other defining factors, companies can provide targeted services catering to the needs of a particular group instead of individuals. For example, if you want to personalize the mortgage home page of your banking application, the first step is to segment the customers as first-time buyers, existing mortgage holders, investment buyers, etc. Existing mortgage holders would be interested in buying a new house or fixing up their existing one, so serving them a page with options to borrow money for home maintenance or porting mortgages would be ideal.

Segmenting caters to the needs of most customers but not all. Segmenting based on one-off impulsive behaviors of a customer, special situations or changing needs can make segmented personalization less effective.

- ***Hyper-personalization***

Hyper-personalization combines behavioral and real-time data extracted from multiple channels and touchpoints to create an extremely customized experience for customers. Hyper-personalization goes beyond just sending an email to the customer that addresses them by their names.

Take, for example, Thread, a UK-based online fashion company which provides personalized clothing recommendations for each customer. Thread asks visitors for gender, favorite brands, preferred looks from a range of images, sizes, date of birth and more. The data collected is used to assemble a picture of the shopper's preferences and provide product recommendations more relevant to the needs of the customer.

Personalization would be exhausting and overwhelming if conducted manually for a huge customer base — if that is even possible. *How is Thread able to do this matchmaking exercise with very few stylists on board?* Answer: with the help of ML algorithms and AI. AI has already transformed many business activities, and personalization is no exception. With AI-driven algorithms, the extent of personalization can be extreme. The key is to limit personalization to that sweet wow spot and not freak out the customer.

- **Over-personalization: Don't be creepy!**

One big complaint people have had with personalization is that it can sometimes feel intrusive. Customers are not happy when personalization goes beyond a certain threshold, especially if they suspect companies have used data that they do not remember sharing or were not willing to share.

For example, Netflix came under fire[105] for personalizing the movie or series artwork based on user viewing history, actor preferences and theme. According to Netflix, instead of showing the original artwork of the film, the tailored artwork may highlight an actor that you favor, capture an exciting moment like a car chase, or contain a dramatic scene that conveys the essence of a movie or TV show.

While this is definitely a fascinating application of technology, it is invasive and misleading. Misrepresenting the content increases the chance that customers will feel betrayed when they start playing the media object.

105   https://deadline.com/2018/10/netflixs-artwork-personalization-attracts-online-criticism-1202487598/

Recommending artworks based on history may not sound alarming, but when personalized technologies are used to make preferences based on places visited, photos posted on social networks, etc., personalization can hit the *creepy zone*.

Sure, AI can learn and predict. But can it be a good artist too? In 2019, the Rijksmuseum in Amsterdam decided to restore "The Night Watch,"[106]a Rembrandt masterwork. The painting had weathered vandalism and a major trimming in 1715 that chopped off its top and left portions. With the help of AI, the missing portions were recreated with amazing accuracy. For the first time in 300 years, the Night Watch is complete again, thanks to AI which can paint like Rembrandt!

---

106   *Artificial intelligence (rijksmuseum.nl)*

CHAPTER 10

PERFECTION

"Quality is the result of a carefully constructed cultural environment. It has to be the fabric of the organization, not part of the fabric." — Philip B. Crosby, Businessman & Quality Management Author

— — — — — — — — — — — — — — — —

The realization that quality is paramount is not new, but many organizations are still playing catch-up. Quality that amazes customers — i.e., that greatly enhances CX — is a long-standing competitive goal. Experiences that amaze the customer are often flawless, with zero tolerance for failures.

In the 1970s/1980s era, North American manufacturers were losing market share to Japanese products. At first, they thought it was because of the price difference, and they did not take it seriously. At first they tried to compete on the price and then they realized it was because of the radical quality control measures that Japanese manufacturers were instituting that made the difference. In fact, Japanese products were popular because they were exceptionally reliable and easy to use.

Philip B. Crosby, in his classic 1979 book *Quality Is Free: The Art of Making Quality Certain*, responded to this quality crisis by advocating the principle of "*do it right first time*" (DIRFT), with expected quality standards being "Zero Defects." Crosby's Zero Defect approach helped to reduce industrial quality issues by 25%.[107]

---

107   *https://en.wikipedia.org/wiki/Philip_B._Crosby*

According to the study done by the Consortium for IT Software Quality (CISQ), the cost of poor-quality software in the U.S. in 2020 was approximately $2.08 trillion.[108] This figure represents cybersecurity failures, operational failures, unsuccessful IT projects and defects in legacy systems. Lack of quality continues to inflict heavy losses and damage to companies across the world.

Defects are a part of life. We all have experienced a sudden car breakdown, a laptop battery running out of juice too fast, apps that crash, walls that crack, etc. *Imagine a world where the products are flawless.* Can we ever achieve this? Humans have striven for ultimate perfection but have fallen short as our intelligence is limited in its capacity to encompass all possibilities in order to avoid failures. With the right quality protocols and technologies, however, have we entered an era where that degree of perfection is attainable?

Quality Transformation

The QA industry, in its constant pursuit of zero-fault excellence, has undergone tremendous transformation in recent years, triggered by several factors: technological advancements, refined development processes and the augmentation of human intelligence. The main trends of this evolution are toward making quality assurance earlier, and faster, and building things right the first time — the old simple DIRFT directive that is so complex to achieve. Having QA mechanisms in place is as essential as ever, but now, to ensure your application always works, you need QA that always is learning and adapting to new development methodologies and customer needs.

---

108   *https://www.it-cisq.org/pdf/CPSQ-2020-report.pdf*

Exhibit 32: Quality assurance transformation

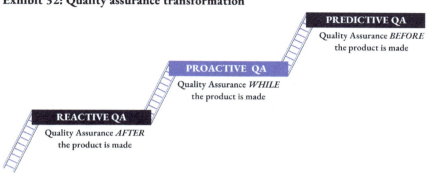

QA has undergone a clear set of stages, culminating in our AI-driven present. The arc is toward applying QA earlier in the software development lifecycle — "shifting left" — as the processes mature. Below are three distinctive stages of QA transformation.

- **Reactive QA**

In the reactive approach, *QA is performed after the product is made.* This method — responding to events after they have happened — was traditionally how QA was carried out. After all, a product needed to be built first before it could be thoroughly tested. The reactive approach was predominantly used in the Waterfall development methodology. It has some advantages: clear deliverables and the value of testing being apparent to all.

But the main disadvantage of this approach is that there is lots of reworking, as bugs are found late in the development lifecycle, requiring numerous iterations back and forth and thus wasted efforts. The end result, in earlier days, was that it took too long to build new features to satisfy customer needs.

- **Proactive QA (shift left)**

In this approach, *QA is applied as the product is being made,* so it focuses on eliminating problems as they appear, before they become embedded in the final product. With competition looming and customers becoming more demanding, there was a growing demand in the 2010s to build new features as soon as possible. Accordingly, the IT world rushed to adopt Agile and DevOps methodologies to accelerate development. QA was forced to "shift left" in the development process and become more proactive. Methodologies like behavior-driven development (BDD) and test-driven development (TDD) hit the field to make QA part of the product much earlier in the lifecycle. And with iterative development and making QA an integral part of the process, it was possible to achieve quality at the needed speed, thus enabling companies to iteratively improve CX.

- **Predictive QA (shift extreme left)**

In this approach, *QA is done before the product is made.* It is based on predictive analytics — the process of extracting useful insights from data coming from various sources by applying statistical algorithms and ML to determine patterns and predict future outcomes and trends. This data-driven technique can be leveraged to predict failure points in testing activities even before the software is made, thus shifting QA to the far left, and minimizing costs while enhancing quality. The emergence of predictive QA was possible only because of a number of technological advancements: AI, ML, NLP, etc. which started to become mainstream in the 2020s.

How to Get to Zero Defects

How can we achieve zero defects in software? While the software testing industry is buzzing with each new framework or tool, human-prone error has always made achieving the zero-defect quality standard (or anything close to it) highly elusive.

Who doesn't like assembling a set of Lego blocks? Lego molds are manufactured to tolerances of 0.001 millimeter to ensure the pieces connect perfectly. The manufacturing process is so precise that it is estimated the defect rate is only 18 bricks per one million made. This exceptional manufacturing process has long continuity: A brick from 1958 is well-matched with a brick bought today.[109]

The rise of smart technology begs the question: *Can AI eliminate human errors and imperfections in software?* When leveraged correctly, AI can provide superior insights on software quality throughout the development lifecycle, but attaining perfection is not a reality quite yet.

The role of quality is evident in the three elements required for continuous, superior CX:

◆ *Predictive quality assurance*
◆ *Predictive maintenance*
◆ *Ensuring availability*

Predictive Quality Assurance

Since ancient times, humans have peered at the sky for guidance, from predicting the weather based on cloud and light patterns to divining the future via the alignment of planets and stars. In our technological world, we derive our predictive capacities from AI and ML, our newfound oracles. Already, AI has proven to be a true boon for humanity in the field of medicine and the aerospace industry. How can this marvelous science be applied in QA? For one thing, the emergent technologies' ability to predict vulnerability is a godsend for quality in almost any industry.

---

109   *https://sites.google.com/view/designandinquiry/case-studies/lego-a-case-study*

Exhibit 33: Impact of AI on test lifecycle

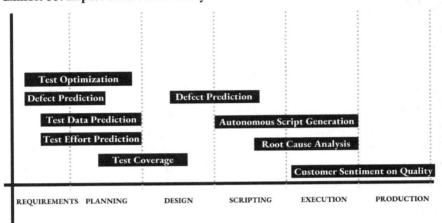

Defect/Incident Prediction

In software development, the aim of QA is to ensure there are very few, or hopefully zero, bugs or other defects in the product. To do so, high-risk components should be identified as early as possible to mitigate risks and reduce costs. An impactful rule in development is that the earlier a potentially defective element is found, the cheaper it is to fix it.

AI-derived defect prediction helps developers focus their maintenance activities on buggy parts of the software. By processing historical incident/defect data, user stories/requirements and software change logs, the algorithms provide useful, actionable insights on the future quality of software. Though this does not eliminate the need for formal testing after the software is completed, it can save a lot of time and money detecting any defect so early in the lifecycle. Efficient ML algorithms are especially useful in situations where problem domains are not well-defined, human knowledge is limited and dynamic adaption for changing conditions is needed.

Optimum Process Flow Prediction

A key step in testing is deriving test cases to identify potential faults. Model-based testing (see Chapter 1) adopts models of a system under test and/or its environment to derive test artifacts. One of MBT's best capabilities is the automated optimization of tests to provide the maximum coverage with the least number of steps.

MBT offers multiple test optimization options which can also be tuned based on additional parameters such as test importance and risk. However, with the introduction of ML, the most optimal path and highest risks can be determined by analyzing the test execution logs and defect patterns from thousands of paths. The paths with the most failures will be prioritized to be executed first.

Risk Prediction

Among the most essential practices of QA is to identify product quality risks upfront and mitigate them. Risk-based testing is the software testing technique that prioritizes the tests of software features and functions based on their risk of failure, importance, and likelihood or impact of failure. This process had traditionally been done manually, with collaboration from the product owner, business and testers to identify risk areas that required mitigation. With smart (i.e., ML-assisted) processing of historic failure data, it is possible to predict accurately which test cases need to be prioritized and executed.

Effort Prediction

In a normal Agile Scrum process, usually the team together estimates the effort required to complete a requirement via planning-poker or on function points. It is a consensus-based estimation methodology, and most often the estimates are the joint *intuition* of the team. However, ML and NLP algorithms allow us to predict the effort required to implement a particular requirement based on past history. The NLP algorithm searches for similar requirements implemented in the past in order to predict the effort of a user story. This is an especially handy technique for estimating a bulk of user stories to decide what would fit in a release and how fast a feature can be realized.

Root Cause Prediction

Root cause analysis (RCA) is a method of problem-solving that tries to identify the underlying causes of faults or problems. The goal is to prevent similar occurrences in the future. RCA was a popular QA technique used in the Waterfall development process to prevent defects. But RCA has fallen out of favor in modern development practices, primarily because it is a manual, time-consuming process. Software defects are fixed and forgotten and very few developers look at the actual cause of the defect. However, AI's ability to predict the root cause of defects makes it highly efficient and brings enormous value to modern development teams, helping them to learn from past mistakes.

Limitations of Predictive Quality

Though predictive QA has driven a revolutionary change in how we think about quality, it comes with its own problems and shortcomings, primarily the following four.

- *Availability of data*

AI thrives on data. The more data fed to the algorithm, the more intelligent and accurate it becomes. While we have huge amounts of digital data available, much of it is unstructured and thus useless for deriving meaningful insights. (While we do not yet have precise benchmark for how much training data is required to render AI useful, it is very substantial.) In most cases, data needs to be preprocessed before algorithms can use it. Complexity increases greatly when data is unstructured, or has a lot of noise. It is often impossible to conclude if a data set will give good results just by scanning the data, so a trial-and-error approach is required to run proof of concepts to check data suitability.

- *Accuracy*

We have precise measures to assess ML accuracy, but it is difficult to determine what degree of accuracy is good enough for a given problem. Especially when ML may be used for predicting life-threatening diseases or mission-critical applications, how much can we rely on its inferences without human interference is a pressing question. It will take some time for people to feel comfortable relying completely on the kinds of machines that are emerging. But it could be seen as merely a change of mindset, considering that we have been comfortably relying on airplane autopilot mechanisms for decades, which is a form of AI. Of course, there is a human to override the computer if needed or to respond to any unexpected situation or condition. Now with self-driving cars becoming ever closer to a wide-ranging reality, this issue is a hot one. It is all a matter of building trust and getting used to the AI/ML algorithmic accuracy.

- *Hardware intensive*

One lever that has triggered the AI revolution is our massive increase in processing capacity. Processing the huge amounts of data that AI demands drives a need for huge amounts of processing power to handle it. Conducting as much computing and storage in the cloud, a highly scalable platform, is one solution that many companies have put in place in recent years.

- *Right use case*

Selecting the right use case — for starters, one that offers maximum benefits without incurring extreme risk — is as tricky as actually implementing the technology. ML is already being used in a wide array of areas, from beer manufacturing to diagnosing diseases, so there are abundant use-case options throughout industries and around the world. One key piece of advice: Always ensure the amount of effort to build a perfect ML model is proportional to the business benefits to be potentially derived from it. Too many companies overinvest in their proof-of-concept models and therefore get underwhelming ROI in their early projects.

Predictive Maintenance

QA, of course, applies just as much in maintaining an application as in building it. It's hardly a new idea: Many industries already use *predictive maintenance* to reduce machine downtime by predicting failures of components or systems. In the interest of cutting costs and reducing downtime, companies have deployed the right blend of sensors and data analytics to enable them to predict which machine parts will fail, and when. Now, with the vast bloom in data and analytics, the same approach can be used for applications before they break down. Though predictive maintenance is not entirely a QA function, QA has a significant supporting role to play in ensuring accuracy of predictions.

- **Aerospace industry**

The aerospace industry is an especially interesting case for those in the QA field. According to Boeing,[110] maintenance and upgrades makes up more than 27% of the total market for commercial aviation services. (Of the remaining 73%, 53% is ground, station and cargo operations, followed by flight operations, with 12%.) In a reactive approach, maintenance problems are addressed only as and when they occur, which is a very costly way to work. In the U.S. alone, the cost of maintenance-related delays for airlines was more than half a billion dollars and one third of flight delays can be attributed to such issues.[111] The main problem from a QA POV is that there exists such an enormous amount of unstructured data in the airline industry. The accuracy of prediction largely relies on structuring the source data and validating its accuracy.

---

110   https://www.boeing.com/resources/boeingdotcom/commercial/market/services-market-outlook/assets/downloads/final_2018_smo.pdf
111   https://pathfinder.datarobot.com/use-case/predictive-maintenance?tab=overview

In fact, the ability to analyze data, find patterns and prevent maintenance failure can transform the entire airline business. Many companies, realizing this, have successfully implemented predictive maintenance strategies that have trimmed the number of cancellations due to maintenance failure and saved millions.[112]

Ensuring Availability

Ever since humans created machines and tools, they have been locked in an eternal struggle to keep them working and continuously improve their performance. Continuous availability of all channels and touchpoints is the essence of positive CX. The use of automation and AI to flag potential malfunctions before they disrupt service is essential to improve application availability.

Getting to Five Nines

Five nines, which means 99.999%, refers to extremely high availability of services, where downtime is less than 5.26 minutes per year. Ensuring such high availability — and reliability — with multiple touchpoints is often daunting and some may argue it is impossible.

Large-scale *resilience tests* with simulated failures are required to ensure there is no disruption of the customer journey. With most cloud providers promising high availability, migrating their infrastructure to the cloud gives businesses the possibility to achieve this feat.

The value of getting to five nines uptime is not just about the promise of availability but it is a way of illustrating service excellence to customers. Especially on mission-critical systems, high availability becomes the most influential CX factor of all.

---

112   *https://www.ainonline.com/sponsored-content/business-aviation/2019-10-18/journey-data-predictive-maintenance*

On Aug. 16, 2013, Google was not reachable for five minutes. In that time, global internet usage decreased by 40%.[113]

Chaos Engineering

Chaos engineering is a disciplined approach to identify failures before they become outages, and such identifications improve system resilience. The technique facilitates experiments to uncover systematic weaknesses. With today's complex systems involving multiple channels and cross interactions, the necessity to improve resilience has never been as great. By reducing the application downtime and preparing the system against unexpected failures, chaos engineering takes you closer to the goal of achieving perfection.

The concept of chaos engineering has been around for years, but it was Netflix that brought it into widespread attention. When Netflix moved from physical infrastructure to cloud infrastructure provided by AWS in 2010, they created the Chaos Monkey — a tool that randomly disables production machine instances. After its success and with Netflix's growing distributed architecture, huge databases and millions of users, chaos engineering evolved into a fault-tolerant system. They believed that they could avoid failures by failing constantly.

Another great example is from Slack Engineering, which aptly terms chaos engineering "Disasterpiece Theater." Since the implementation of chaos engineering, it has identified serious vulnerabilities to the availability or correctness of Slack before impacting customers. According to Slack's Richard Crowley, chaos engineering has greatly improved the app's reliability and confidence in its fault tolerance, thereby improving customer trust.[114]

---

113   https://www.gosquared.com/blog/googles-downtime-40-drop-in-traffic
114   https://slack.engineering/disasterpiece-theater-slacks-process-for-approachable-chaos-engineering/

> *Instead of avoiding failures, chaos
> engineering embraces it.*

This technique sounds interesting theoretically, but it begs many questions. We need to look at the concrete details of applying it, in order to answer the chief question: *How do you implement chaos engineering in your organization?*

Prerequisites of Chaos Engineering

For chaos engineering to work for your organization, it is essential to have a clear purpose. Companies like Netflix and Über have implemented this approach, but not without doing their due diligence.[115] Trying to implement something as complex and cutting edge as chaos engineering without the right preparation risks more outages, dissatisfied customers, broken products and annoyed management. So we recommend paying close attention to all the following key prerequisites.

- *Impact analysis*

Simply pulling the plug off a server is not chaos engineering; it is just chaos. Obviously, a proper *impact analysis* is needed before embarking on the journey of chaos engineering. The nature and business-criticality of the application in question looms large in determining which experiment to execute. For example, when certain Netflix services are down, it causes some user inconvenience and perhaps annoyance, but it is hardly life-threatening. In industries like medicine, space and finance, more elaborate impact analyses are absolute prerequisites.

- *Preparation for failure*

Chaos engineering entails its downsides and limitations, such as needing to face small and large failures. No matter how many impact analyses you do or the number of precautions you take, there is always

---

115   https://spectrum.ieee.org/chaos-engineering-saved-your-netflix

a chance that your experiment can go wrong. The issue is not *if you will fail,* but rather *when you will fail.* Failing earlier in smaller steps is much better than complete failure or shutdown later.

- **Incident management & response**

Even a carefully planned chaos engineering project is bound to cause some disruption in application operations, so it is vital to have a mechanism to spot the failures as soon as possible and have an incident response team in place to fix such issues as soon as they occur.

- **Continuous monitoring**

The capacity to observe and monitor how your application reacts to chaos is the most important prerequisite. Without such visibility, it is impossible to determine whether the intended experiment has met its objective. Monitoring must be foolproof and end-to-end, because the introduced chaos sometimes has "side effects" that influence unexpected parts of the application.

Chaos Engineering Steps

With all the prerequisites in place, it is time for action, proceeding along the following steps.

- **Define the hypothesis**

First, ask: *What could possibly go wrong?* Record each failure your team highlights and make a backlog of all chaos experiments you want to conduct. For example, a hypothesis can be, "When the xyz microservice fails, the users should still be able to access the basic features of the app."

- **Select & prioritize the experiment**

With the risk analyses done, plot impacts against likelihood of occurrence. The experiment with the highest impact and greatest likelihood of occurrence will be the obvious choice to be picked up first.

- **Conduct the experiment**

Failures can't be prevented but the risk can be mitigated. The experiment is to be run automatically, in an environment as close to production as possible, ideally after every change.

Chaos experiments need especially close management. Keep the "blast radius" at a minimum if possible, limiting it to only very few customers — with a rollback mechanism in place if the experiment gets too risky. Carefully choose the timing of the experiments to avoid risky periods when most users access the application.

Like many other modern software development practices, chaos engineering demands a mindset change. While in conventional projects, robustness, stability and stringent change management processes are preferred over disruption, with chaos it is just the opposite.

The following are the most common attacks simulated with chaos engineering.

Resource constriction: One of the principles of chaos engineering is to seek how the application will respond to unavailability, or minimum availability, of resources like CPU, memory, etc. This can be simulated by generating high loads on CPUs, allocating only a minimum percentage of RAM or generating traffic to write to disks.

Network constriction: Distributed systems rely on external dependencies over the network for successful operations. What happens if the network is unavailable or does not perform at the desired level? With external dependencies, it is critical to understand the impact.

Black hole: A black hole, or packet drop, is a type of denial of service attack in which a router that is supposed to relay packets discards them instead. It is a great way to test application behavior under latency or from failure of a specific network component.

Domain Name System (DNS) blocking: One of the foundations of the internet, DNS converts human-readable domain names into Internet

Protocol (IP) addresses. By blocking DNS, the application's behavior is validated during internet failures.

Change of state: How does the application behave when something in the app's environment changes, such as a shutdown, restart or killing of a node in the server? Change of state can also be simulated by changing the system time, killing the process, etc.

- **Scale or squash**

It is a good thing if the experiment did not go well — that is the whole point. You probably found a bug and tested the failback mechanism. If not, increase the blast radius or choose another experiment to repeat the process until every potential soft spot is tested and verified.

When Escalators Break, They Become Stairs

Even with all built-in quality gates in place, it is unavoidable that a strange incident will someday occur which your application does not handle. How do you manage these issues? *What happens when your application fails?*

As a design principle, the idea of failing gracefully is worth pursuing. Take the example of escalators: Even when they break down, they still are usable but in a less efficient way. The same principle should, ideally, apply to your application as well. With the right decoupled architecture and design, it is possible that customers are able to use the application even when some parts fail or become unavailable.

In an internet banking application, for example the whole application does not go down if the transaction module becomes unavailable. Customers can still view their account overviews and existing transactions.

A clear message informing users about the failure and the expected period to resolve it will go a long way in maintaining an acceptable CX. A step further would be to email or message customers as soon as the issue is resolved. Analytics and personalization can help in achieving this.

CHAPTER 11

CONTACT

*"A computer would deserve to be called intelligent
if it could deceive a human into believing that it was
human."* — *Alan Turing*[116]

- - - - - - - - - - - - - - - - -

We all know by now the sense of delight and ease that voice-controlled smart devices afford us when we ask to hear music, find out the weather or answer our questions. This technology, which has been in the market for years now, continues to evolve day by day.

We have come to take these capabilities for granted, so they fall short of the "wow" threshold. But machine-human communications, especially as mediated by NLP, certainly holds much wowing potential, as these interactions become more effective, impactful, "intuitive" and rewarding.

In fact, with the right quality systems and standards in place, this technology can *entirely change the way businesses interact with customers and solve their problems.* For one thing, customers increasingly demand access to information and solutions to their problems at any time of day, and they expect a quick response to their queries. Voice-activated technology is the perfect answer, once some quality hurdles are overcome.

---

116   https://mathshistory.st-andrews.ac.uk/Biographies/Turing/ quotations/#:~:text=A%20computer%20would%20deserve%20to,that%20 needs%20to%20be%20done.

We also all know how frustrating it is to receive inadequate service. Companies lose over $75 billion a year due to poor customer service.[117] When a customer is in distress, how well you respond and how you treat them makes an immense difference to their experience and thus their loyalty to the company's products or services.

So, what is the ideal CX for help and question resolution? Simple: "Someone" being available to help you and resolve your problem in an instant. That someone need not necessarily be human, but must *seem* like it is, in terms of responsiveness and comprehension.

Contact Centers Lead CX

The contact center, also referred as the customer interaction center, is the central node where all customer contacts are managed. This is why it is essential to create a service culture there that enables employees to translate customer contacts into satisfying experiences.

The reality of contact centers has evolved to keep pace with the times. For one thing, there was a time when telephone interactions reigned supreme in interactions with the customers. But times have changed and customers have a wide variety of interactive channels to choose among like email, chat, social media and smart devices. And the contact center is where all these touchpoints and channels are integrated into one platform for omnichannel customer support. Experts agree that usage of new channels on smart devices and social media will only continue to increase,[118] and so the conventional quality measures to assure call quality and interaction are no longer sufficient.

117   https://www.forbes.com/sites/shephyken/2018/05/17/businesses-lose-75-billion-due-to-poor-customer-service/#56530c0e16f9
118   https://www.smartinsights.com/social-media-marketing/social-media-strategy/new-global-social-media-research/

Exhibit 34: Impact of contact center on customer experience

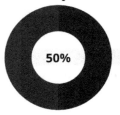

50%	66%	94%
Investment projects directed to customer experience innovations	Customer experience is influenced by providing accurate and effortless interactions	Contact center leads overall Customer Experience transformation

Time seems to be speeding up every day and our collective insistence on speed and efficiency is reaching extreme levels. The younger generations especially expect tasks to be accomplished with ease and immediacy.[119] The now-familiar railroad-station and fast-food kiosks serve as examples of the trend where self-service technology is outpacing human interactions for efficiency and even CX as a whole.

With self-service, customers can resolve their own issues with little effort. Many people even prefer self-service to talking to a human agent. And emerging technologies hold great promise in making this a reality. But for complex interactions, it remains necessary for a human agent to intervene in order to ensure customers get what they want. On the whole, the balance between self-service vs. human interactions will swing further away from human involvement.

To provide this front-line support, companies increasingly use AI-assisted tools like *chatbots*. Unlike humans, chatbots keep a consistent mood, hold no personal biases and work 24/7 with no coffee breaks. The success of these virtual assistants has led to the explosion of chatbots across industries. According to Cognizant, the global chatbot market is expected to reach $1.25 billion by 2025, growing at a CAGR of 24.3%.[120]

---

119   https://chainstoreage.com/what-attracts-younger-shoppers-kiosks
120   https://www.cognizant.com/us/en/archives/whitepapers/documents/the-future-of-chatbots-in-insurance-codex4122.pdf

Exhibit 35: Banking channel evolution

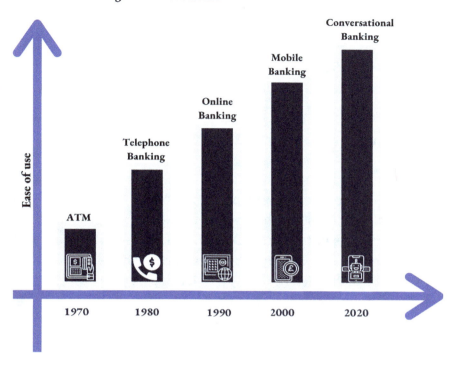

CX failures are likely to occur when customers switch channels, especially between self-service and human agents.

Using AI comes with a ton of benefits but can also pose potential dangers to the society and the individual customers using it. A good example is the AI chatbot released by Microsoft on Twitter. Within a day, it developed some offensive habits.[121] Without proper risk identification and mitigation, this can happen to your chatbot as well.

Ensuring Quality of AI-Assisted Bots

For AI-assisted technologies, quality is a game changer that facilitates their evolution into more and more reliable providers of superior CX. QA for chatbot requires specialized knowledge and a particularized

---

121 https://www.theverge.com/2016/3/24/11297050/tay-microsoft-chatbot-racist

skill set. Handling uncertainties and unknowns in a chatbot interaction requires a mix of traditional QA and an AI-based approach.

QA for customer-assistant bots starts with these basics:

◆ *How chatbots work*
◆ *Challenges of testing chatbots*
◆ *What needs to be tested?*

How Chatbots Work

A chatbot or chatterbot is a software application used to conduct an on-line chat conversation via text or text-to-speech, in lieu of providing direct contact with a live human agent.[122] As noted above, chatbots are poised to revolutionize how companies interact with their customers, allowing organizations to deepen the conversation and evolve the customer/company relationship as they deliver world-class CX. Interactions can take a vast array of forms, as AI provides the flexibility to cover any subject area with customers — such as feedback on purchases, information on demand, answers to problems, etc. Chatbots have the ability to greatly advance the conversation with customers and thereby serve as a strategic differentiator.

> 😊 Short Bytes
>
> *Back in the mid-1960s, Joseph Weizenbaum at the Artificial Intelligence Laboratory at MIT invented ELIZA, which is considered the first conversational chatbot in history. ELIZA's answers were so convincing that when chatting with her for the first time, some people thought they were talking to a human therapist. But ELIZA's responses were determined solely by a series of scripts and pattern-matching.[123]*

---

122   https://en.wikipedia.org/wiki/Chatbot
123   https://en.wikipedia.org/wiki/ELIZA

Chatbot Architecture

Exhibit 36: Chatbot architecture

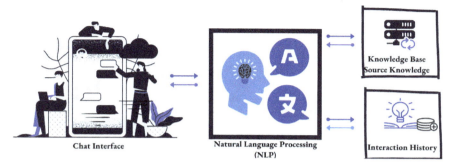

| Chat Interface | Natural Language Processing (NLP) | Interaction History |

- ### *Speech recognition & text conversion*

For bots — which are like a new species of entity that can understand our speech and respond in kind — the speech-to-text conversion process begins with automatic speech recognition (ASR). ASR is the technology behind services such as Amazon's Alexa, Apple's Siri and Hey Google. The first step is to collect the audio through a microphone and filter out any background noise. In the next step, ASR decodes the acoustic features into probable words. With more training and usage, the bot learns the nuances of speech patterns of an individual user and gets better in recognizing the person's speech.

- ### *Natural language processing (NLP)*

The aim of NLP (which we have mentioned earlier in the book) is to use the words extracted by ASR to derive semantic information and meaning. To extract meaning from the text, the words are organized in structured grammatical objects. These grammatical objects are then used to find out the "intent" of the conversation — i.e., what the user wants the bot to do. While building the bot, programmers defined the intents as logical actions or tasks that the bot can perform. For example, with a flight-booking bot, the questions asked by the users can be interpreted as below.

User Utterance	Intent
Book a flight to New York	*Booking*
Give a list of flights to New York	*Inquiry*
I am thinking of going to New York	*Inquiry*
The last flight I booked to New York was horrible	*Feedback*
Reserve a ticket on the earliest flight to New York tomorrow	*Booking*

Table 3: Utterance and intent mapping

- ### *Response generation*

Once the bot understands what the user is asking for, the next step is to provide an appropriate answer to the question (or implied question). The response generator takes interpreted intent and context as input and generates a response to the user. Before forming its response, the generator considers: (a) the knowledge database with predefined and learned responses for a particular intent, (b) a dialogue history database and (c) an external data source with additional intelligence.

For example, there are predefined libraries that can be deployed within the bot application to engage in small talk. With its predefined "small talk" library, the bot has immediate access to replies to conversations about the time of day, the weather, etc.

- ### *Management of conversations*

Once the chatbot has chosen a response, the next step is to determine an interaction strategy — i.e., who is leading the conversation: the user, the bot or both parties? A bot-driven conversation is "safer" than a user-led one, as users often provide ambiguous, ill-defined inputs which can lead the bot to a different conversation than the intended one. A bot-driven conversation, however, restricts the interaction and tends to become boring and flat. A mixed conversation is ideal, where both sides move the conversation ahead.

Can your next lawyer be a Chatbot?

In 2015, *Joshua Browder created the world's first robot lawyer –DoNotPay. In the first 21 months since the free service was launched in London, Browder says DoNotPay has taken on 250,000 cases. The program first works out whether an appeal is possible through a series of simple questions, such as were there clearly visible parking signs, and then guides users through the appeals process. It has now developed into a million dollar company with a huge customer base.*[124]

Challenges of Testing Chatbots

Quality control for AI requires a completely different approach and mindset than traditional QC. Below are some challenges that you will find in testing AI.

- *Nondeterministic inputs & outputs*

A nondeterministic algorithm provides different outputs for the same input on different executions. Humans are nondeterministic by nature: We could provide different answers to the same question, depending on our mood and circumstances. NLP algorithms, developed to mimic human language patterns, are trained to frame and construct their own responses based on continuous learning.

- *Language variations*

One of the biggest advantages of chatbot technology is its ability to understand a vast panoply of languages, including many dialects and local variations. This enables multinational companies to connect with their customers worldwide. While multilingual support is a great feature to offer, it poses unique challenges for QA. To start with, finding people

---

124   https://donotpay.com/

with multiple language skills in different geographies is a challenge. Automation of QA requires special language adaptations as well.

- **Linguistic variations**

Linguistic variation refers to the variation in which a specific language is used because of regional, social, contextual or grammatical differences. As we know, in conversation language can be used in multiple different ways. For example, if you want to ask the digital assistant about the weather for tomorrow, you can pose the question in a number of ways: *How will the weather tomorrow be? Will it rain tomorrow? Do I have to take my umbrella tomorrow? Can you tell me the forecast for tomorrow in Celsius?* The conversation bot must be able to interpret and provide correct answers to all these questions which have the same intent.

- **Chatbot personalities**

Chatbots are perhaps the best examples yet of the human quest for *anthropomorphization* — to endow nonhuman entities like machines with human traits, emotions and personalities. And without some semblance of "personality," conversations are insert and dull. This applies to bot talk as well, and is why companies such as Microsoft and Google are hiring novelists, playwrights and comedians to build their conversation platforms and make them more interesting for customers. Some factors, such as sarcasm and irony, are especially challenging for testers due to their subtlety and complexity, but they must be considered as well.

What Needs to Be Tested?

Chatbot and digital assistant (DA) capabilities are relatively easy to create, compared to traditional programming, because much of the logic happens through ML. Numerous platforms are available in the market that make creating smart assistants simple and easy. There are also some poorly conceived DAs in the market. A malfunctioning DA can induce bitter CX and reputational loss for a company.

> *"I know that I am intelligent, because I know that I know nothing." – Socrates*

▪ Measuring intelligence

Measuring human natural intelligence is a tricky, complex and vexing matter fraught with issues such as accounting for educational level and social conditioning. Measuring machine intelligence is nearly as complicated. However, the "intelligence" we measure in DAs is a narrow, service-level intelligence, not the capacity to concoct new philosophical theories or compose a beautiful song. To measure the artificial service intelligence of your smart speaker app or chatbot, the following scoring matrix is a good start.

Skills	Skill Specifics	Description	Score
Ability to Understand	Text recognition	Ability to process text inputs and infer their intended meanings	
		Ability to understand abbreviations, short forms, spelling errors, emojis, etc.	
		Ability to understand phrases, idioms, sarcasm, etc.	
	Speech recognition	Ability to understand human speech and digital voices	
		Ability to understand accents, dialects of a language	
		Ability to filter noise and identify conversations	
	Action recognition	Ability to differentiate conversations from call for action commands	
	Emotion recognition	Ability to understand emotions of the user from texts or through speech inputs	

Ability to feedback	Contextual response	Ability to interpret the context and provide feedback	
	Textual response	Ability to interact with the user through textual conversations	
		Ability to adjust volume, switch voice and accent settings	
	Speech response	Ability to interact with the user through voice	
	Video response	Ability to play the right video requested by the user	
	Image response	Ability to communicate through right contextual image	
Ability to learn		Ability to remember the preferences and choices of users	
		Ability to recognize a user from voice	
		Ability to frame responses based on continuous learning	
Personality		Ability to exhibit a personality	

Table 4: IQ scoring for smart bots

- ***Does it always work right?***

Perhaps the most awe-inspiring attribute of AI technologies is their ability to improve continuously by learning. This amazing human-like feature can also be its biggest downfall if not controlled properly. Because of bots' continuous learning, one that works perfectly today may not work well tomorrow. It is necessary to continuously assure the quality of the bots to avoid any mislearning.

- **Testing the intents**

As discussed above, "intent," in the chatbot world, represents the purpose of a user's input. An intent is defined for each type of user action your application supports. Validating the user's intent means understanding exactly what the user wants to know.

- **Accents & dialects**

Every person has an accent (regardless of whether or not they think they do), and an effective chatbot needs to accommodate all the different possible pronunciations in order to maintain accuracy. And our species' linguistic diversity is staggering, with roughly 7,100 spoken languages on Earth today and nearly countless dialects.[125] English alone is spoken in 160 distinct dialects throughout the world, including 29 distinct dialects in England itself.[126] All these variations in human communication demand a fully thought out strategy for testing bots using at minimum the most used and supported dialects and accents.

> ☺ Short Bytes
>
> *Human voices are hard to mimic. Even with the latest technologies, it is impossible to match human speech except for short conversations. In 1846, in London's Egyptian Hall, something truly bizarre was on display for people paying a shilling. Joseph Faber's invention, the Euphonia, was the first known robot that could mimic and replicate human speech. It is reported that it took Faber seven years just to get the machine to pronounce the letter "e."[127]Many observers of the machine found it unsettling or creepy.*

---

125   https://www.infoplease.com/world/social-statistics/how-many-languages-are-there
126   https://www.lingohut.com/blog/so-how-many-english-accents-are-there-in-the-world-the-number-may-surprise-you/
127   https://newspunch.com/meet-euphonia-the-victorian-text-to-speech-robot-from-1846

- *Chat language, typos, errors and abbreviations*

Social media is having a clear impact on our written language. A soup of acronyms, abbreviations and neologisms has been cooked up to speed the need to communicate faster and minimize the inconvenience of typing on small mobile devices. The problem with these abbreviations is that they are not standardized and they can take on different meanings, dependent on the context and domain in which the chatbot is used. To add to the complexity, we are increasingly expressing our emotions through emoticons. Does your chatbot understand these newly invented conventions? Can the bot understand nonverbal communication? Can it understand human emotions through symbols? Can it autocorrect obvious mistakes and typos? We need to answer these questions before a chatbot is ready to serve.

- *Response times*

Nobody likes to speak to a laggard bot that takes too long to respond. After all, performance is the prime factor driving the experience of using a chatbot. However, lightning fast responses are disorienting to users, as they create the sense of pre-selected responses, which is impersonal. It is essential to maintain the conversational momentum at the right pace.

- *Multichannel compatibility*

Because users nowadays have come to expect omnichannel support, chatbots need to be available on multiple channels. The only way to ensure perfect availability is through testing the bots for compatibility to ensure similar look and feel, responses and error-handling across channels.

- *The Turing test*

In 1950, Alan Turing famously raised the question, "Can machines think?" He sought to find out if machines can be as intelligent as humans are, and therefore he introduced the "imitation game" (now called the Turning test). In this test, the same question is asked both to the machine and a human being, and if a human evaluator cannot reliably tell the difference between the response from a machine and that of a human, the machine is said to have passed.

Turing tests are still relevant today for modern chatbots, because what they measure is an integral part of CX. Customers should never get the feeling that they are talking to a dumb machine that cannot understand their problems and feelings. Though the overall chatbot interactive experience should be similar to that of speaking to a human, the European Union draft regulations (at the time of writing this book) state that the end customer should be made aware that that they are speaking to a machine and not a human.

- **Testing the limits**

Most of today's DAs are designed to handle predictable situations and normal human behavior. *But how would they cope with irrational situations?* This occurs to many users who are inclined to test conversational AI's limits by asking the same question over and over again, or even posing meaningless or obscene questions. By doing a limit test upfront, the digital assistants are tested for all fallback scenarios and irrelevant questions. The optimal way to check most scenarios is to use a request generator — with a mix of sensible and irrelevant questions.

CHAPTER 12

INCLUSION

"Just having satisfied customers isn't good enough anymore. If you really want a booming business, you have to create raving fans." [128] *—Ken Blanchard, Motivational Author & Speaker*

- - - - - - - - - - - - - - - - -

While we all have seen the effects of disastrous *mass thinking*, in politics and other world events, it is a given that the crowd possesses better judgment than the individual. Indeed, it is a foundational principle undergirding democracy. (And when crowd thinking goes amiss, it is often due to the extreme effects of ideology or propaganda, rather than an aggregate of individual foolishness or malevolence.)

In general, the crowd is usually right when no external factors are influencing them. This is evident from the game show, *Who Wants to Be a Millionaire?* When an individual is asked a true or false question, the chances for getting it right is 50%. When the same question is asked to the crowd, the chances of their getting it right are much higher. Even though some of the individuals in the crowd just guess, their collective judgment is always better than that of a single person.

In his 2004 book, *The Wisdom of Crowds*, James Surowiecki argues that the aggregation of information in groups often results in better decisions than if made by a single member of the group. *How does this influence CX? Is your collective customer pool a "better judge" than your architect or designer? How can you assemble a functional*

---

128   https://www.azquotes.com/quote/695684

crowd that represents your customer base? Can you use the power of crowd in your design and development activities? All these questions point to shifting left CX.

How to Shift-Left Experience Assurance

Shift left is about bringing solutions closer to the customer. Even before the product is launched, we need to think of how people will react to it and what will be their emotions when using it. The best way to achieve this is by involving the customer in the design, development & assurance process. Shifting left by involving customers in the development process is a three-step undertaking:

- ◆ *Design thinking with customers*
- ◆ *Right deployment & testing strategies*
- ◆ *Assurance by customers*

Design Thinking With Customers

As both an ideology and a process, *design thinking* is concerned with solving complex problems in a highly user-centric way — a form of cocreation. This is in stark contrast to the traditional approach of creating solutions based solely on a company's sense of what is needed in the market. Design thinking brings customers back to the center of the technology journey — where they belong — and helps organizations design brand-differentiating experiences that keep pace with real-time consumer expectations and needs.

Exhibit 37 shows the five stages of design thinking, all of which warrant a deeper dive.

Exhibit 37: The five phases of design thinking

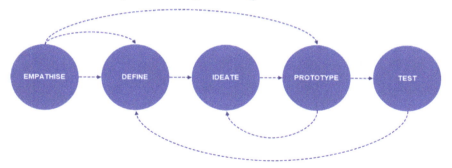

- **Empathize**

Empathy, the capacity to understand or feel what another person is experiencing from within their frame of reference, is a human trait that not everyone possesses in large measure. Nevertheless, some empathy usually can be acquired through practice. And practice consists of *listening in order to understand others' needs and problems and then jointly defining what a good experience is.*

Having a customer journey map (see Chapter 7) at this stage provides a deeper understanding of customers' motivations, frustrations and travails at every step of their journey. It is worth spending considerable time at the empathize stage to thoroughly understand customer requirements, which all subsequent stages are based around.

- **Define**

During the define stage, the team gathers concrete ideas and formulates smart solution themes as defined by the *problem statement.* A good problem statement is broad enough for creativity, yet specific enough that the challenges at hand are truly addressed.

- **Ideate**

The third stage is about generating as many ideas and potential solutions to the defined problem statement as possible. You need not always look internally for the best ideas; customers often have creative solutions to their own problems. Tapping customers' ideas not only helps in shaping the solution but also increases their loyalty, as they have a sense of ownership when their ideas are respected and implemented.

- **Prototype**

A *prototype* is an early sample, model or release of a product built to test a concept or process. With the wealth of digital prototyping tools available in the market, it is now fairly easy to create clickable proofs of concepts that allow customers and stakeholders to get a look-and-feel sense of the future product. A perfectly designed prototype is one that is imperfect. Prototypes are designed to capture failures early and inexpensively. Design is an iterative process, and smart prototyping helps bridge the gap between ideas and actual customer needs.

- **Test**

Although customer testing is the final stage of the process, in an iterative process testing often leads to redefining problem statements or realizing more features. This phase enables the development team to see where their prototype fares better and worse, before sinking enormous amounts of energy, time and money in a given project. Based on customer feedback, the prototype can be further enhanced at this stage, or a completely new idea might emerge. Creating multiple prototypes with simple variations can be revealing for determining customer preferences.

Airbnb, a leader in online vacation rentals, was once on the verge of bankruptcy with revenue barely reaching $200 a week. It was saved by pure design thinking. By putting themselves in the shoes of the customer, the Airbnb team found that the problem was the poor quality of pictures uploaded by the customers who placed ads. The photos, which were taken on smartphones, were not attracting enough viewers and were not clear enough for end consumers to see where they would be staying. By sending photographers to the homes of people placing ads, Airbnb was able to double revenue immediately. They learned a valuable lesson of seeing through the perspective of the customer in their design process. A nontechnical/ non scalable solution that did not involve any code saved the day and created a fabulous company.[129]

Deployment & Testing Strategies

Involving customers in the development process is easier said than done. Two key moves for customer invovlement are to break down new features into smaller chunks that could be easily verified and establish the right deployment strategies.

Canary Deployment & Testing

Everyone knows about the "canary in the coal mine," how the small songbirds were used as sentinels to indicate the presence of noxious fumes in mines because they succumbed before humans. Well, in software development and testing, *"canaries"* are simply small features that are deployed in production usually to a smaller user group to find out how well the features perform. After a successful canary — measured against KPIs like performance, usability, etc. — the user group is expanded iteratively

---

129   https://review.firstround.com/How-design-thinking-transformed-Airbnb-from-failing-startup-to-billion-dollar-business

Blue Green Deployment

Blue green deployment is a technique to reduce deployment outages and risks. Two identical instances of production run in parallel environments. One is the "green" environment, which hosts the current production version and the live traffic. The new features are first deployed in the "blue" environment, where smoke tests are run to ensure that the desired functionality works well. The blue environment can also be opened up to test with a small group of customers before switching the live traffic to the blue environment.

Though this deployment strategy looks logical and allows a fail-safe approach for deployment, it requires good infrastructure to make it happen. It's also important that all pending transactions are dealt with before making the switch to this method. Maintaining data synchronization and integrity in real time would be a major challenge with this approach if not done correctly.

A/B Testing

A/B testing, also called *split testing*, is a method of comparing two variations of an application to determine which one performs better. The variation is usually not the whole website but rather one or more page elements like a button, text or image. The A/B testing technique is one of the handiest options for marketers who are working on conversion rate optimization — i.e., getting users to take the next step, whatever that is: clicking a button, buying a product, signing up for a newsletter, making a call, etc.

For example, in 2012 Barack Obama created history again by being the first candidate ever to receive $1 billion in donations, raised mostly through online campaigns. Over 500 tests with different combinations of page elements like images, buttons, text, etc. were run to arrive at the page with maximum conversions. In an example quoted by Kyle Rush, the engineer who worked on the campaign, the website first just had the picture of the president on the donate form. However, when an inspirational quote was added, like, *"Stand with me, work with me, let's finish what we started!,"* the conversion rate rose by 17%.

Despite A/B's popularity, proper planning and technology assistance is required to carry it out. The first step, as usual, is to define the purpose and clear objective of the A/B testing. Do you choose to test your new features, or elements of marketing like campaigns, posters, etc. Once you have decided what you want to A/B test, you need to run the variations in parallel.

- **Create an A/B test plan**

Having a good test plan gives a head start in making your A/B tests successful. An A/B test plan should have a properly defined goal and specify the means to achieve it. It should consider the target audience involved in the A/B tests, splitting the traffic, usage of the tools and the duration of the tests.

- **Define success**

Define success based on straightforward questions such as: *What is the purpose of the website? What do you want to achieve with this A/B test?* Then translate the answers into quantifiable success metrics.

Defining success is easy for most websites and features. For example, if A/B testing was done for a fundraiser website with a "Contribute" or "Make a difference" button — the obvious metrics will be the number of clicks (the first "conversion") and then the conversion rate for actual contributions. As more features and variables are added and tested for complex business models, defining success criteria can become progressively more involved.

A/B testing can be carried out for a wide variety of business objectives such as measuring page views, donations, lead generation, number of conversions, form completions, etc.

- **Define the hypothesis**

The next step is to define what you think you will find in the experiment. Hypotheses help to refine your success criteria by providing more information and assumptions made for the experiment. A/B tests stem from the desire for improvement, so your hypothesis statement should clearly include what you want to improve and by what means.

- **Measure the outcome**

Measuring the success of A/B tests depends on their objectives. Most tests include customer engagement like the number of clicks on a page, number of people signing off and other conversion rates — and eventually success should contribute to monetary benefits.

Multivariate Testing (MVT)

Multivariate testing is an extension of A/B testing, wherein you make changes to multiple sections or features of your webpage/app and evaluate which set of variations out of all combinations provides the best CX according to subjects' feedback.

For example, if you are building a website for a charity organization and you are undecided on what quote to use and what image to use to drive donations, you can use multivariate testing to find out what works best. These would be the variables:

Quotes: (Quote1, Quote2)

Image: (Image1, Image2)

Button: (Donate, Contribute)

With these three parameters, you can devise eight (2*2*2) different variations, or versions of your website. You would then expose the variants to equal numbers of customers to find out which version has the best conversion rate.

This methodology works well for Agile teams where customers are involved quite early in the process before rolling out an update or a new patch. Of course, too many variations would make the process too complicated and unfruitful. Once again, it is a question of finding the sweet spot for testing.

Beta Testing

Beta testing uses actual intended customers to validate the CX while using the product. It is conducted when the product is 90- 95% complete. Real-time usage can find the bugs and issues that eluded the grasp of the designers, developers and testers. Beta testing can also be used as a marketing ploy: It helps to create buzz among customers about the new features even before they hit the market.

Assurance by Customers

It is not enough if you involve the customers in the design and development processes. Involving customers in the assurance process is essential to bring in the real user perspective. Following are ways to include customers in the CX journey.

Crowd Experience Assurance

Crowd experience assurance is a practice that harnesses the efficiency and advantages of crowdsourcing to get direct feedback from the crowd on their experience of using a particular product or feature. The wisdom of the crowd applies to CX as well.[130] The perception of experience and quality could vary from individual to individual. However, when asked for collective feedback, it is easier to interpret what the majority of your customers really need. In other words, crowdsourcing closes the gap between your *perception* of customer needs and the reality.

---

130   *https://www.applause.com/*

How can you engage the crowd to provide feedback? While crowdsourcing sounds great in theory, making it a reality is the trick. To do so, we need to ensure the right infrastructure, the right crowd, the right incentives and a mechanism for collecting feedback and reflecting on the results. Those are the basics of any crowdsourced strategy.

- ***Platform for crowd assurance***

For crowd testers to operate efficiently and effectively, a simple user-friendly platform is required. Besides enabling people to participate, the platform should also have a mechanism to report bugs, track activities, communicate with task owners, etc. The platform should comprise the following elements:

1. *A portal to post the project, relevant documents and expectations from crowd testers.*
2. *A chat mechanism for crowd testers to communicate among themselves and with the task giver.*
3. *A defect management system to register the crowd testers' findings.*
4. *An administration mechanism to register new users and take up new tasks. Crowd testers should have access to users' account information along with the rewards offered.*

- ***Choose a diverse crowd***

Depending on what is being tested, it is generally best to crowd-test products on people with diverse backgrounds. Ideally, the crowd will blend those who are long-term customers and know much about the product with new customers who have no such knowledge, and

---

131   https://www.toyota-global.com/company/history_of_toyota/75years/data/ automotive_business/products_technology/vehicle_lineage_chart/trademarks_ and_emblems/index.html

perhaps a group of quality engineering professionals — people specialized in the technology and the product. If the product is used in many countries, it is good to involve people from all geographies with the right distribution.

- **Localization**

While a diverse crowd brings different perspectives, conversely it is also sometimes important to localize your target crowd. A product that is very popular in the U.S. could be literally unknown in China. So target your crowd test campaign based on the demographics of the product usage with the localized profile, language settings, etc.

- **Incentives**

For most people who participate in online crowd testing, the basic motivation is monetary. A modest money reward and prizes in exchange for completing tasks can motivate the crowd to participate actively. Other than monetary benefits, competition and recognition among the community can help drive people. The tool of gamification, if used wisely, can provide an immersive experience for the crowd and motivate people to participate.

- **Moderate the results**

It is imperative to moderate the findings of the crowd testers, and to do so as soon as possible to keep the community of testers active and interested. It is a tedious process to validate all the findings of the crowd testers and classify them as bugs, duplicates or irrelevant. An efficient way to do this would be to crowdsource this task as well. Making a few of the regular crowd testers "super users" or moderators will take the burden off from having to hire a moderator.

Crowd Benefits

- **Experience on real devices**

Crowd testing provides cost-effective access to a wide range of devices, browsers and operating systems. Working in a lab, there are nearly inevitable app crashes from some test participant who uses an odd hardware/browser/OS configuration. Such risks are minimized with crowd testers because they just use their own device configurations to test, which provides better coverage than the emulation and virtualization used in device labs.

- **Customer perceived quality**

The insights provided by a fresh pair of eyes are quite valuable. Often the crowd testers do not hunt for the technical correctness of the application as they may not have a deep understanding of the product. The usability and design problems are the first things that surface, when people outside the project look at it. It is important not to dismiss these findings but to encourage and tap into these insights to provide valuable experience to the end customer.

Types of Crowd Testing

Desirability Testing

Desirability testing is a set of research methods that assess target customers' emotional responses to a design, feature, product or service. This type of testing is done by providing participants with a pile of sticky notes or cards with a range of positive, neutral and negative adjectives written on them. The cards are placed randomly on a table and then customers are asked to pick three or four that best describe their emotions when watching the demo of a product or feature. When done with a minimum of 25 participants, this exercise offers excellent insights on customers' emotions while using the product (which is a long way of saying CX). The results can then be analyzed by simply calculating the percentage of positive versus negative responses or building a word cloud with all responses to see which emotions are stronger.

Desirability testing is also called the Microsoft Reaction Card Method, as it was first developed there and documented by Joey Benedek and Trish Miner in their Usability Professionals Association 2002 paper,

"Measuring Desirability: New Methods for Measuring Desirability in the Usability Lab Setting."[132]

Exhibit 38: Product reaction cards

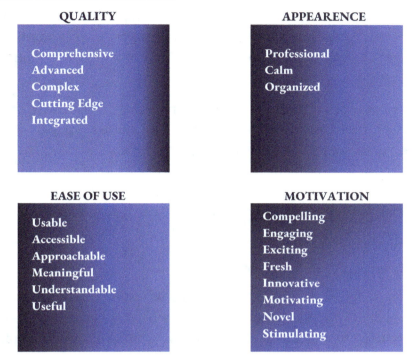

QUALITY	APPEARENCE
Comprehensive	Professional
Advanced	Calm
Complex	Organized
Cutting Edge	
Integrated	

EASE OF USE	MOTIVATION
Usable	Compelling
Accessible	Engaging
Approachable	Exciting
Meaningful	Fresh
Understandable	Innovative
Useful	Motivating
	Novel
	Stimulating

Focus Groups

Well known in popular culture, *focus groups* are used in testing nearly anything: tv shows, political speeches, household products, etc. They can be a powerful tool for bringing out customers' spontaneous reactions and for gathering instant feedback to find out customer needs, wants, difficulties, etc. Focus groups often consist of six to nine customers that experience a product and discuss their issues and concerns about it. The group is typically run by a moderator who maintains their focus.

---

132   https://www.researchgate.net/publication/228721563_Measuring_
Desirability_New_methods_for_evaluating_desirability_in_a_usability_lab_setting

Card Sorting

The *card sorting* user research technique allows testers to discover how users expect to find your content presented. It is a great way to learn how customers perceive the logical relationships among the various elements of your app, and yields insights on how to best organize a website or software application so the structure of information will be logical for the largest number of users.

In the card sorting process, a participant is given a number of cards (or notes) containing different themes, topics or words, and then is asked to sequence the cards in a logically suitable manner. The test is performed with multiple types of customers, and the most common perceptions are derived. This information can then be used in the creation of navigational elements or the structuring of information.

Card Sorting Details

- *Open and closed card sorting*

Card sorting can be open or closed. Open gives more freedom to the participants. In addition to grouping the cards, they can also define the categories that make sense to them. This type is best to understand how users would group your content.

In closed card sorting, the categories or labels are predetermined. This exercise helps to understand how users fit content into an existing structure. For example, in an e-commerce website there could be existing categories: garden, electronics, toys, sports, etc. When the company introduces new products, it can use closed card sorting to determine customers' thoughts on which category the new wares belong in.

- *When is card sorting useful?*

Card sorting can be used in many situations, such as designing a user-friendly business process, structuring the presentation of content and improving labeling. The most common usages include:

- o   *Classifying products*
- o   *Determining the sequence of steps in a process*
- o   *Untangling complexity*

- **Finding participants**

Selecting the right set of customers for CX validation is harder than one might assume. Card sorting is ideal for smaller groups with lots of interaction and gamification. To select ideal participants, first create detailed and specific persona descriptions. Also, incentivizing participation with gift cards or other monetary rewards always helps.

Crowd Limitations

- **Confidentiality**

Great ideas and features need to be validated and crowd testing is a great way to get real feedback. However, the problem with the public crowd is that you are not in control of who has access to your ideas and new features that you want to experiment with. Your competitors would also get the first look on where you are heading.

- **Legal and Security Policies**

Legal and security policies impose restrictions on crowd testers to access applications. Also, providing correct test data can be a huge challenge. Companies often use real customer data, which is often risky to share with the public even in an anonymized form.

POSTSCRIPT

I hope these past pages will prove helpful and valuable to you by offering perhaps a different and more holistic model of the CX journey — one showing how integral a role quality plays in every facet.

For anyone in the quality profession, or IT in general, these are heady times where old ways are swiftly giving way to new realities. To be prepared for the future, it is now imperative for IT and quality professionals to keep on growing, continually, in technical expertise and experience. As quality and QA professionals acquire new skill sets and training, they will need to unlearn old ways dependent primarily on individuals' experience and assessments. Immeasurably powerful algorithms are already making many quality approaches obsolete, and there's no turning back. Meanwhile, with work increasingly augmented by technology, specifically human skills will be in high demand: creativity and critical thinking skills, which machines are not good at, will be the roles for tomorrow's workers.

The advent of AI and other smart technologies is fascinating, and will certainly be an agent of massive change within our profession as well as every other field. Quality is automating rapidly and in doing so is transcending previous paradigms of what it can accomplish. Old, manual quality processes are being phased out and replaced by cutting-edge, technology-assisted approaches.

Dovetailing with the era of smart technologies is the age of digital data in which we now find ourselves. In fact, in the last couple of years humans have produced more data than in the entire history of humankind. Such an upsurge in data is already changing every industry and job, and people in widely dispersed disciplines find themselves needing to become "data scientists" in order to keep up.

While the juggernaut of technology can appear to be an out-of-control train, we in QA must be intent on keeping the vehicle on its tracks

— and not getting run over ourselves. Moving forward, technology will no longer remain the domain of the few, but the province of the many. With technology, the future is neither gloomy or dark, but rather an unfolding way of life. The relationship between humankind and technology is set to change the world as we know it.

www.ingramcontent.com/pod-product-compliance
Lightning Source LLC
LaVergne TN
LVHW051639050326
832903LV00022B/812